Annihilate
Stress and Anxiety

21 Proven Strategies for a Balanced Life

Merryn Snare

Global Publishing Group
Australia • New Zealand • Singapore • America • London

Annihilate Stress and Anxiety

21 Proven Strategies for a Balanced Life

Merryn Snare

DISCLAIMER

All the information, techniques, skills and concepts contained within this publication are of the nature of general comment only and are not in any way recommended as individual advice. The intent is to offer a variety of information to provide a wider range of choices now and in the future, recognising that we all have widely diverse circumstances and viewpoints.

Should any reader choose to make use of the information contained herein, this is their decision, and the contributors (and their companies), authors and publishers do not assume any responsibilities whatsoever under any condition or circumstances. It is recommended that the reader obtain their own independent advice.

First Edition 2014

National Library of Australia Cataloguing-in-Publication entry

Snare, Merryn, author.
Annihilate stress and anxiety : 21 proven strategies for a
balanced life / Merryn Snare.

ISBN: 9781922118448 (paperback)

Stress (Psychology)--Prevention.
Anxiety--Prevention.
Stress management.

616.85223

Published by Global Publishing Group
PO Box 517 Mt Evelyn, Victoria 3796 Australia
Email info@GlobalPublishingGroup.com.au
For Further information about orders:
Phone: +61 3 9739 4686 or Fax +61 3 8648 6871

DEDICATION

I dedicate this book to my delightful daughter, Laura, whose love, support and generosity of heart, mind and spirit is my inspiration, and to my late parents Olwyn and Wes who always gave me unconditional love and support and encouraged me to achieve my goals. And finally, to my late husband Bruce, who always believed in my ability to achieve my goals and make a difference.

ACKNOWLEDGEMENTS

Whilst my purpose in writing this book has been about encapsulating my professional experience and transforming it into print, I have been fortunate to have met many wonderful people along the way – clients and colleagues alike. I would like to thank them all for sharing their wisdom and perspectives with me. I would also like to acknowledge the support and guidance offered by friends and colleagues which has been so generously shared with me throughout my career; in particular Joseph Gagliano, Maryla Juchnowski, Rosi Bullock, Maureen Hay and Paula Saltalamacchia.

I also acknowledge the work done by ADAVIC (Anxiety Disorders Association of Victoria), Beyond Blue and Sane, all of which contribute significantly to the area of mental health in our community. From a broader perspective, I would also like to mention the work of Oprah and Dr Phil, who through their media platforms have assisted in raising the profile and importance of mental health care across the globe.

To the various mentors who have offered their guidance, I thank them for their inspirational insights, and to the Global Publishing Team, whose guidance and support made this project a reality.

Finally, I make special mention of my editor, Laura Macintosh, whose willingness and enthusiastic support has made this project even more rewarding.

FREE BONUS OFFERS

Valued at $157 but yours

FREE

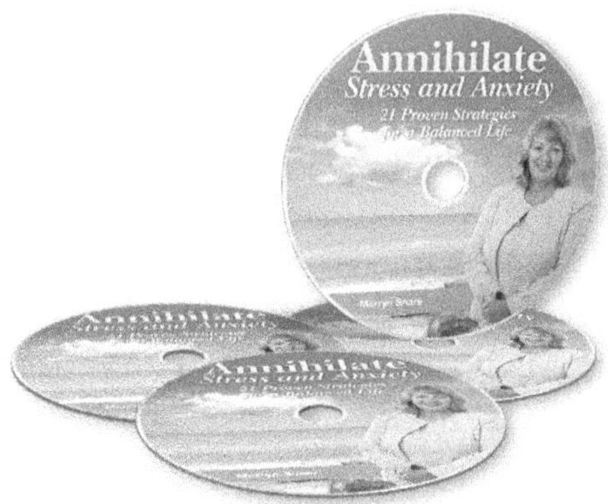

As a special bonus GIFT, I am also offering you a special audio recording of **five instant stress-busting strategies.**

Try them out – see how you feel when you empower yourself to take charge.

Claim your

FREE BONUS GIFT

by going to

www.AnnihilateStressAndAnxiety.com/bonus

TABLE OF CONTENTS

INTRODUCTION

The Prevalence and Pervasiveness of Stress and Anxiety

Whilst most of us are well aware that stress is a fact of life, it seems that much time and energy is consumed by this natural phenomenon in a negative manner. Whilst stress in its acute form can be exciting or motivating, like the adrenaline rush experienced by the thrill of a physical activity, for example jumping the wake on skis behind a speedboat, riding a jet-ski, hot-air ballooning, or being a spectator at a tense match of your favourite sport; this level of excitement or stress is not sustainable indefinitely, and hence, constant stress becomes a burden. Added to this are the demands we place upon ourselves – expectations that we would never expect of another, and yet we tend to beat ourselves up if we do not achieve the 'greatness' that our minds have conjured into a raft of high-performing and high-achieving expectations. When we leave these expectations and demands unchecked, they are likely to lead to more serious mental illnesses, such as anxiety and clinical depression, and yet if caught and treated early, stress and anxiety is very treatable.

A recent study commissioned by the Australian Psychological Society to examine the status of wellbeing of Australian adults found that twelve percent of adults experienced extremely severe stress[1]. In addition, one in three was found to suffer depressive symptoms (with 10% of these being in the severe range) and one in four suffered anxiety symptoms (9% of whom fell within the severe range). The Australian results were

found to be similar to studies conducted elsewhere in the western world, including the USA and UK. The concerning feature of these studies is that stress is on the increase, and if twelve percent are suffering severe stress, the numbers suffering stress significant enough to impact their quality of life is likely to be far greater. This survey found the primary sources of stress to be financial issues, personal health, family issues and the health of others, and 30% of people cited work-related stress. The impact of stress is wide-reaching; it affects our physical and emotional health, and often shows up in maladaptive behaviours if not treated and taken seriously.

A timely reminder: if *you* do not, will not or cannot look out for *you*, who will?

Stress is also having a social impact on society, as reported by a study conducted by The Emily Post Institute in Boston, U.S.A. This study followed a survey conducted in 2005, when on examining questions of etiquette it was found that 69% of participants believed Americans were ruder than previously. Curious at this seemingly high figure, the author was keen to re-test the social climate and found a resounding 82% of participants believed that American society was ruder than previously. Whilst the 2008 recession was largely blamed for adding stress to people's lives, it was concluded that stress and rudeness present in a recurring cycle. Much post-recession stress was linked to workplaces downsizing or closing their doors, but once again the role of technology emerged. Organizations keen to work smarter are using technology with increasing sophistication, whilst workers are under increasing pressure to 'do more with less'[2]. Once again it becomes evident just how difficult it can be to separate the causes of stress, with causal factors occurring both within and external to the workplace.

Considering that mental health issues such as stress and anxiety were barely acknowledged 20 years ago, it is clear that our society has

significantly improved its understanding of the importance of these issues. However, although we better accept and acknowledge the importance of mental health as the underpinning of sound health in general, so has our lifestyle become more complex and demanding. Whilst technology and the field of medical science has made many wonderful advancements, so too has it made life more difficult and stressful.

In short, most people seek to realize their potential, and to do this they need to be able to manage their competing priorities in order to work productively and make a contribution.

So what is it that gets in the way?

Stress!

In most cases, it gets back to learning how to understand the role and impact of stress and to identify and manage or alter the stressors that create one's stress.

Why this book?

My intention in writing this book is to create a practical handbook for readers that provide explanations and strategies to enable them to understand and better manage stress and anxiety. My big hope is that this will help people to understand stress, how and why they react to it, the uncomfortable side effects that accompany it, and to learn how they can manage and take control of it, becoming more resilient, and enabling them to enjoy life rather than allowing stress to dictate.

Before proceeding further, I should be clear about what this book is not. It is not a literature review detailing the latest research. Whilst research and reviews of such have a very important function and as a psychologist was the foundation of my training, this is not what I am setting out to do. Nor is this book a comparison of different psychological approaches. It does not compare or evaluate, nor does it tell you the pros

and cons of one psychological approach over another. It is a book which outlines the tools, strategies and methodologies that I use regularly in my clinical practice, and which seem to provide positive outcomes for those who implement them.

Understanding how and why stress and anxiety develop, and why they escalate causing discomfort to the point where it impacts ones quality of life, is a crucial first step in building personal resilience. We need to understand that stress and anxiety are common and 'normal' events, but we should also be aware that when stress diminishes our quality of life rendering it less enjoyable or fulfilling, or when it marginalizes us in some way, we need to do something about it.

The tools and strategies I outline in this book have been tried and tested in my clinical practice over many years by my clients. They are techniques that I find to be simple, but effective; I believe simplicity is essential if people are serious about enhancing their coping strategies or modifying their behaviours. If the strategy is complex and too time-consuming, when under pressure it becomes too difficult to remember what to do, how to do it, or even to do it all. The most difficult part is remembering to 'Do It'.

Hence, my goal for my clients, and you, the reader, is to assist in building your own personal toolkit of strategies to enable you to manage the daily ebb and flow of stress and anxiety. There will naturally be some strategies in this book that you enjoy or find easier to implement than others, which is absolutely fine. It is about filling your toolkit with as many strategies as possible and then working with the ones that you find most effective for the situation at hand.

This is not intended to replace professional treatment for severe stress, anxiety or depression, but if you adopt your personal combination of strategies early, you are better placed to prevent many stress situations

from becoming overwhelming, thereby annihilating stress and anxiety before it gets a grip!

So, what does it require from you? The first step is that you have bought this book – and I thank you for that – but really, the first decision is to adapt your behaviours and thought patterns by adopting the strategies that best suit your needs. From there you need to take action. Read the book, look at the strategies, try them out, and work out which ones suit your personality and your lifestyle. Which are the ones that you can implement simply, easily and regularly? Which strategies can become a part of your response mechanism? From here you need to practice your strategies regularly to have them form a part of your thinking and behavioural routines. This will not only provide you with the confidence of knowing you can manage any stressful situation you may encounter, but also builds your resilience, an extremely valuable life skill.

A word of warning here: these strategies are unlikely to come naturally to begin with. Like any new habit, it takes time to build them into your repertoire. You will need to constantly remind yourself to implement the strategies you choose. This is normal. Most people find they are not as diligent or able to remember to include their new best intentions initially, and need to work at establishing a system or routine that will remind them about our new behaviour-response system. But it is not difficult, so persevere. I invite to read on. Enjoy. I hope you find this book useful, which is my number one intention. Step one is to get started: 'having a go' is a great effort and a really good start to establishing this new response set.

Before long you will be well on the way to annihilating stress and anxiety.

Part 1

THE 'HOW AND WHY' OF YOUR MIND

A strong positive mental attitude
will create more miracles
than any wonder drug.

Patricia Neal

CHAPTER 1

What is Stress?

Stress is all around us. It is very much a fact of life and some people believe they need stress to function properly, but what is stress? The meaning of stress originates from an engineering term relating to the load that a structure can take before being compromised and when such compromise occurs, there is usually some form of collapse. For people, the stress is usually emotional or psychological rather than physical and the collapse relates to an inability to function via our cognitive mechanisms. Hence, stress is generally defined as the imbalance between the demands on one's resources and their ability to meet these needs. The impact of human stress however, whilst initially relating to one's emotional and psychological functioning, also impacts physical functioning and individuals who find themselves in a place of being completely emotionally and psychologically overwhelmed will struggle to function properly in any capacity.

If we are aware of the potential disaster that may arise from such imbalance, we might ask how and why we allow ourselves to get to this point. Perhaps we think – or hope – that we are super-human and have a limitless supply of resources, or maybe we are simply unaware of when our resources are being stretched to breaking point. It might also be that we don't know how to refresh our resources regularly to avoid such collapse. The real answer lies in the fact that our stress build-up is a culmination of our individuality; our personality, our unique and personal coping styles, our thinking patterns, and our life experiences.

Some people insist that stress is a positive thing and that they perform better when under pressure. Somehow, they feel they lack the drive to achieve or complete tasks without the push of pressure. In essence, this is true and the type of stress they are referring to is called *eustress*. This is the form of stress that motivates us and pushes us to keep going or achieve more and most of us can relate to experiences where eustress has assisted in our achievements.

More often however, we hear about negative stress, or *distress*, which does not help us at all. This is what weighs us down, drains our confidence and erodes our self-esteem. The real key is to understand our own unique balance between *eustress* and *distress* and perhaps more importantly, to understand what contributes to this balance being tipped.

Individuality and Stress

It is not unusual to find that several people who all experience the same stressful situation can have very different stress responses, thus highlighting the influence of our individuality. In essence, individuality combines personality, genetic predisposition, environmental influences, life experiences, and our cognitive structures or thought patterns. The scope for such wide variations between individuals across so many factors is indeed a significant element in the frustrations some scientists face in their acceptance of psychology as a science – it is impossible to be precise, which is why when investigating elements relating to psychology and human behaviour, we need to focus on trends.

Personality

Personality is often the first broad reason given for such differences in people's differing reactions to stressful situations, but what is personality? The most frequently used definition of personality refers to the *Big Five* personality factors taken from the *Five Factor Model*, which have been described in several forms by numerous researchers[3]. The *Big Five* factors include:

Openness to experience: being inventive and curious, rather than consistent and cautious. This factor measures traits such as appreciation of the arts, curiosity and sense of adventure, willingness to engage in a variety of activities rather than being routine, and cognitive experiences using imaginative and independent thought.

Conscientiousness: being efficient and organised, as opposed to carefree and easygoing. This trait reflects self-discipline, focuses on achievement, and is typified by calculated rather than spontaneous behaviour.

Extraversion: tending to take charge and enjoying excitement. This trait is one of positivity, energy, assertiveness, sociability and the desire to seek the stimulation of others.

Agreeableness: being friendly and compassionate, rather than cold and unfeeling. The tendency is towards compassion and cooperation, rather than being suspicious and antagonistic towards others.

Neuroticism: being sensitive and nervous versus secure and confident. These people tend to be more vulnerable to the negative emotions of anger, anxiety, depression and vulnerability, as opposed to feeling stable and secure.

On a personality assessment, each of these factors is determined by a set of questions designed around the behaviours and views encapsulated in each measure. Each factor is considered as a continuum, with individual traits on each factor falling at some point along that factor's spectrum. In other words, individuals are not seen as being totally one extreme or another but are rather their unique and individual blend of elements within the factor scale. Whilst they possess traits from each side of the continuum, individuals are ultimately more inclined to one side of the scale than the other, e.g. the degree of neuroticism or negative emotion exhibited versus the degree of optimism and positivity they display. When we hear people described as 'glass half full' or 'glass half empty', it is an indication of how they perceive negativity and positivity, or where they believe they fit on the neuroticism scale.

Many of us are keen to know whether our personality should be attributed to our genes or our environment. Whilst twin studies suggest that genetic and environmental factors have a similar degree of influence on personality, with genetic influences accounting for approximately 41%–61% of

traits on the *Big Five*, it is interesting to note that personality tends to stabilise once adults settle into the workforce[4]. This is understandable given that workforce entry usually coincides with the ultimate transition from adolescence to adulthood. Although some studies defined adolescence as nearing its conclusion around the age of 18 years, my personal view is that particularly in developed countries such as Australia, with the majority of students completing year 12 before going to some form of further tertiary training, be it university, apprenticeships or anything else in the workplace training arena, the adolescent period extends to approximately 25 years of age. I find that between the ages of 15 and 18, students are highly focused on their schooling. At the age of 18, when most students leave school, they encounter many forms of freedom all at once. In Australia they reach the legal age for voting, drinking, gambling and in the state of Victoria, driving. They are also in higher learning settings where the discipline to turn up for class, hand work in, sit tests, exams and the like, is completely up to them. What's more, unlike the nurturing model of secondary school, there seems to be limited support for those having difficulty with this adjustment, which is arguably one of the most significant adjustment periods in their development. The time I believe individuals make the transition from adolescence to adulthood is this period when most students have completed their vocational studies and are moving into the workforce. This supports the notion that personality stabilises after approximately four years in the workforce. Once students have left school and university, they tend to form friendships with people of like mind, values and ethics, rather than with the classmates who just happened to be there. To a large extent, I feel that school peer-group formations are a matter of luck – who was there to choose from when making or selecting new friends from in your class or year level or school?

Many of these personality scales alter with maturity, which is when personality traits settle. For example, people tend to become more agreeable and less determined to get their own way as they mature. But of course, there will always be exceptions to the rule!

Thinking Patterns and Coping Styles

We are all individuals and our personality has bearing on how we think, how we perceive stimuli and how we interpret the impact. To some extent we learn these response styles from key people of influence, largely our parents and other close family members, or friends, teachers, coaches and also celebrities and sports stars whom we either admire or aspire to be like. The key personality factors also have a profound effect on how we think – whether we are an extrovert or tend towards neuroticism. Are we laid-back, easy to get on with and agreeable, or does our conscientiousness drive our need for good results or perfectionism and influence how we respond? What becomes pivotal to our response mechanism however, before events are even categorised as stressful, is the way we interpret the situation. This critical factor then becomes our *belief system* – what do we *believe* the outcome of a situation may be? This opens up avenues of positive or negative outcomes, which sets the domino effect of our response mechanism.

When we combine these elements of individuality, we come to understand the importance of our *belief system,* which has a major influence on how we respond to stress and helps to explain why people react to the same stress stimulus in so many and varied ways. These are broadly individual circumstances but the takeaway point from this relates to the individuality and uniqueness of our perception – how we, as an individual, *interpret* something and how we *think* about it, together with how we *experience* something and *respond* to it.

The ABC Model of Thought Processing

The ABC model of thought processing was founded by Aaron T Beck in the 1960's. His work with patients experiencing depression led him to the conclusion that negative thoughts were the basis for many issues. His work became known as "cognitive therapy", and attracted much attention

within the field. Beck's approach was later expanded and became known as "cognitive behaviour therapy" or CBT[5]. The ABC model illustrates the pivotal role our beliefs have in our thought processes, and that recognising our *belief structures* and evaluating their impact is essential to understanding our propensity for developing mental stress and anxiety. From here we are well placed to determine whether changes to our belief systems are possible, or indeed necessary.

Often referred to as the ABC model, A refers to the *activating* event or situation to which one is reacting, B represents our *beliefs* about that event, usually in relation to the direct impact it has on the individual, and C refers to the *consequences* or behaviours that result from the combined impacts of A and B.

In the example below, Mary is upset because her friend, Katy, has not returned her phone call.

A ⟶ **B** ⟶ **C**

Activating Event	**Beliefs**	**Consequences or Outcomes**
Friend fails to return a phone call.	They are trying to avoid me.	Distress at the thought of being disliked. ↓ – Lowered self-esteem – Hurt (emotionally) – Anger – Denial – Thoughts of retribution – Social withdrawal

In this example, had Mary used these alternative thoughts, the outcome might look more like this:

A	B	C
Activating Event	**Beliefs**	**Consequences or Outcomes**
Friend fails to return a phone call.	1. Perhaps she didn't receive my message. 2. I wonder if she is on holidays. 3. I hope she and her family are well and there is nothing wrong.	I will call again.

The key to managing our stress reactions can therefore be said to lie within our belief system and this is where our personal work must begin. This too is easier said than done, as changing our life-long belief blueprint is no easy matter, but the good news is that it can be achieved! Research into neuroplasticity of the brain – the ability of the brain to adapt and change – reveals extremely positive results regarding the brain's ability to expand itself and retrain or change the way it sees things[6,7]. Hence, we know that we are able to change our existing behaviour patterns and moderate them or mould them into more productive ways of being.

The impact of stress is therefore likely to vary from one person to another, with the reasons for experiencing excessive stress relating to a complex combination of individual thinking patterns about life experiences. However, there are elements in our daily living that we all have

in common. Life is full of ups and downs, which I refer to as *big S and small s* stresses, many of which we are able to manage. For example, a *small s* stress might be a frustrating drive to work whilst a *big S* stress might be getting stuck on the freeway on the way to the airport, resulting in you missing your flight. In essence, *big s and small s* stresses are pertinent to you, and usually reflect what is happening or important for you at the time. Stresses like a chaotic drive to work, a family problem, or an underlying work problem that has been bubbling away for a while can all add an unwanted level of pressure. This might be capped off by someone cutting in front of you whilst driving, or arriving at work to find you have forgotten your entry pass. The tipping point or the final straw that sees your *stress hill* become an erupting volcano might, on its own, be quite minor, however if it is part of a build-up, and it may be sufficient to push you through your *coping ceiling* to the point of meltdown, where your resources at that point in time are inadequate, rendering you unable to cope.

These stressors occur each day and build into what I refer to as our *stress hill*. It is when the stresses of this *stress hill* build to the point where our coping resources are exhausted, that we reach emotional exhaustion – or meltdown. What makes it difficult to monitor where our stress level is at, is the fact that it often creeps up slowly without us noticing. To compensate, we put an additional effort into our daily tasks, which might be so small that we don't notice its impact initially. Over time, however, things tend to change. As pressure builds, our ability to manage it begins to diminish and it is only after time has passed that we notice things have changed, often significantly, and we don't feel the way we used to; we experience more headaches, our body generally aches more from increased tension, our mood fluctuates, we forget things or mess things up way more that we used to, and we feel cranky with everyone and everything much of the time. Then we begin to feel freaked out and think "What is happening to me?!"

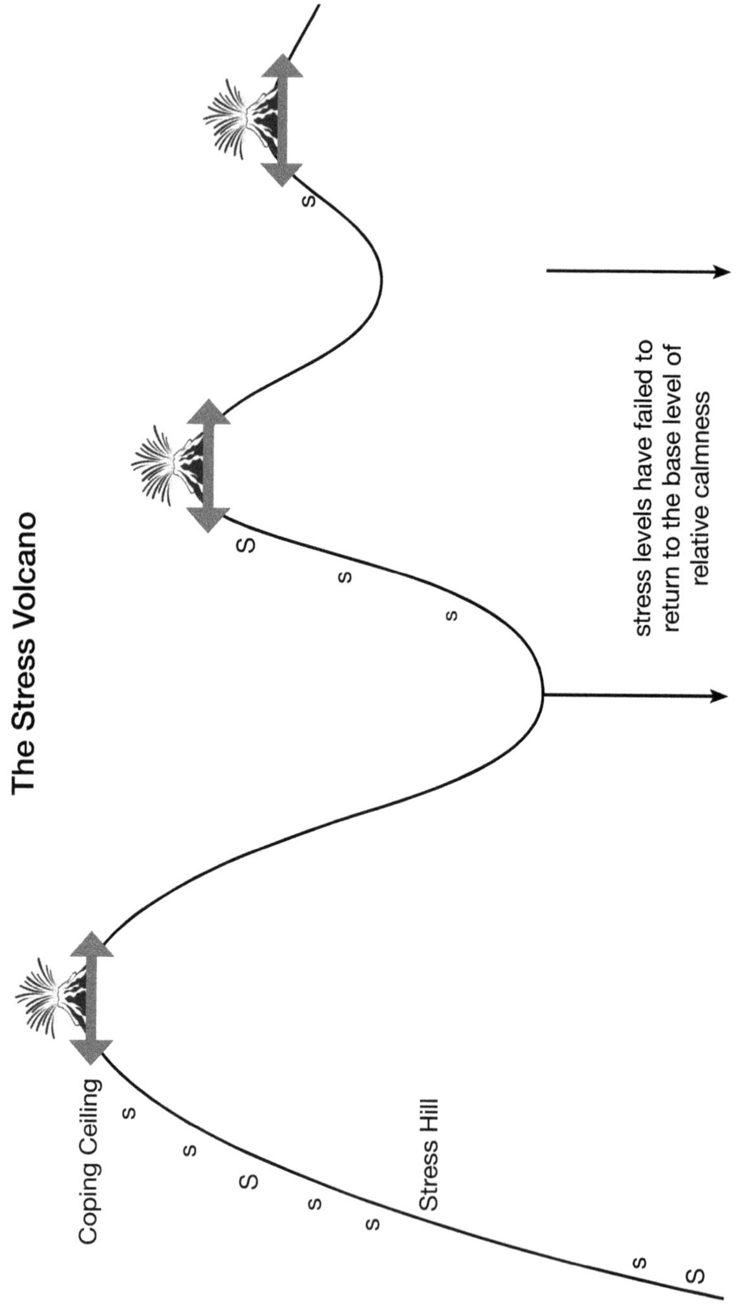
The Stress Volcano
Coping Ceiling
Stress Hill
stress levels have failed to
return to the base level of
relative calmness

Have you experienced this?

I refer to this as the *stress volcano* and the diagram explains how the volcano builds to the point of eruption.

The *stress volcano* shows how *big S and small s* stress reactions build our *stress hill.* There is no particular order and no particular rhyme or reason.

After bursting through the limits of your coping resources – your *coping ceiling*-for the first time, one tends to feel some relief. This is most likely a combination of both physical and emotional relief as the tension within has finally found a way out, enabling a chemical reaction in the brain where endorphins are released and which assist the body and mind to recover. Emotional tears often result from stress, and they release the natural painkiller **leucine-enkephalin,** which improves mood and assists the body to feel better. Hence, people who have a crying response often report feel better once this release has occurred[8].

Adding to our confusion following the erupting *stress volcano* is the fact that we often can't explain to anyone – let alone ourselves – what is happening. Those around us notice, but are perhaps too scared to say anything for fear of causing further distress. It is frustrating when we just cannot put these feelings into words, yet we know something is not right. Because we are unable to articulate what is happening, we then resort to enforcing those incredibly high expectations we have of ourselves – perfectionism, being a super-mum, super-dad or purely super-human. We may even start comparing ourselves to friends, family members and colleagues, celebrities or sports stars – if they can do this, so *should* I.

Have you ever experienced this?

This is the beginning of a spiral that usually winds in a downwards direction and takes us to a psychological place that is uncomfortable and unpleasant. The notion of 'should' is an important element of self-talk to be aware of as it is a blatant clue about where your thinking is heading – and remember, as pointed out in the ABC model, it is your thinking that

has a major impact on kick-starting the stress wind-up. Your thought processes are pivotal in the stress cycle and in the next chapter I will discuss more about the role of thought patterns in this downward spiral of stress.

All human beings are born with emotions, both positive and negative, and most of us are quite clear that we prefer the positive ones. After all, who wouldn't prefer happiness and excitement to sadness and dread? An important purpose of emotions, however, is to give us an indication of how things are impacting us – what we like and what we don't like. We should also be tuning in to how we are feeling so that we can gain an indication of where our stress levels are at. To assist us here, keeping a close eye on our daily functioning, our diet, and our exercise and sleep patterns can forewarn us of an unhealthy stress build-up.

So how do we deal with excessive stress? Firstly, we need to look at what has been changing in our world. The difficulty is that these changes usually occur slowly over time and we often don't notice them until we are struggling, to the point where our performance has diminished. However, the short answer is that we need to change. Just what we change is a matter of personal analysis.

The first part of the personal analysis is to do a self-audit. Look at the commitments, activities and routines in your day or week and note what you enjoy. If you don't enjoy much at all, consider what you used to enjoy and ask yourself whether you are still doing it or why you don't enjoy it any more. Look at what is different from before you were aware of this stress build-up and consider what you might need to change to get back to a place of equilibrium.

Past Experiences

The extent of our exposure to perceived difficult situations and events, the time in our life such events occurred, and the support mechanisms we had to assist us in coping, are all likely to impact our response to stress at any given time. For example, young children are usually protected

from harm by their parents and caregivers, as even with relatively minor painful events that they might encounter, such as bumps, trips and falls, there is usually someone there – a protector – to sooth and support. Depending on how they are supported will influence the resilience skills they develop for later in life, and those who are sheltered and protected from all types of harm will have little opportunity to develop and test their ability to cope. On the other hand, for those who have grown up in war-torn environments and face severe stress on a daily basis, whilst initially their responses might be one of extreme anxiety and fear, over time they may become used to their environment and react less. This is not to scoff at those who become stressed at seemingly minor stressors – it is all about the individual's perception, which tends to be at least partially influenced by their previous life experiences (or lack of experience), and is not for others to judge. Remember, our perception is our reality.

Significant Stress Events

Critical Incidents

Another potential influence of past experiences occurs when individuals are exposed to, but are unable to cope with, a major impact event, such as being involved in or witnessing a workplace accident that causes significant injury, or the witnessing of any incident causing harm to others. The nature of support services available following a critical incident varies, depending upon circumstances. For example, most workplaces provide Employee Assistance Programs (EAP) for employees, and sometimes their family is also included. This enables access to limited counselling for any issues. As an extension of the EAP there is usually a critical incident service, where counsellors are available to support staff who have been traumatised following a major impact event or critical incident. The usual process is for counsellors to attend the episode immediately, to provide psychological first aid and follow up with additional sessions to check on the recovery, and provide information for people as they move forward. After this initial intervention, rather than seeking additional

assistance or support, individuals tend to push the experience away without acknowledging its impact or their resulting feelings, and hence, don't properly deal with it. This is common and people often believe that by pushing the stressor or situation away they are 'coping' or 'dealing' with it, until another significant stress event occurs, reminding them of the initial one they believed they had dealt with. The subsequent event tends to elicit similar emotions to the first or previous experience, linking the person to memories of the event they believed they thought they had dealt with. After critical incidents, I have often had people say, "It is just like when … happened. I feel exactly the same, but I dealt with that – it happened years ago!" But did they really deal with it?

My contention is that when people have experienced something awful and they (perhaps understandably) do not want to feel the discomfort of the negative emotions that must accompany a negative life event, their primary focus becomes taking away the unpleasant feelings. Often the quickest and easiest way of achieving this is to push it aside, bury it, or cover it up, so you no longer need to pay it any attention. This might work with minor events and it might also work for a while following a significant traumatic event, but when it is pushed aside, I think of it as being buried, and like a weed in the garden; it grows roots, and before you know it, you are overwhelmed by it again.

Post Traumatic Stress Disorder

Post Traumatic Stress Disorder (PTSD) occurs when someone, who has experienced a significant or terrifying event, does not recover as easily as they would like. Whilst humans tend to be generally resilient to life's difficulties and challenges, some might experience a negative event that has such a major impact that they do not recover easily which, in turn, can have a significant impact on their quality of life. Typical symptoms include nightmares, intrusive thoughts, flashbacks, avoidance of talking about the event and/or of visiting locations near where the event occurred, hyper-arousal, or severe anxiety. These symptoms may

manifest behaviourally; by the person becoming irritable, having difficulty sleeping, or being hyper-sensitive to sounds or smells; indulging in self-destructive behaviour, such as increased drinking, smoking or use of illicit drugs; or cognitively, with ruminating thoughts, difficulty concentrating or memory lapses.

The symptoms of PTSD may come and go and may be triggered by an innocuous and unrelated event. For example, I was speaking with a young man who told me that he was born in Afghanistan and the family moved to Iraq when he was very young to escape the difficulties of war. Five years later, when he was still at primary school, the family moved to Australia. Now in his 30s, this man is well educated, involved in his community, and highly regarded in his workplace. He relayed a recent event of his involvement in a charity sporting match where, as a part of the festivities, the police air wing came to show the children the helicopter. As he heard the chopper overhead, he described how he experienced an almost overwhelming emotional response that surprised him and took him back to his early childhood. Whilst this man's reactions to this event did not lead to major psychological trauma, he was surprised that after such a long time (since being exposed to the difficult conditions in the Middle East) the impact of traumatic situations can reappear in the most unexpected of situations.

Vicarious or Secondary Trauma

Vicarious or secondary trauma is perhaps more common but less understood. Potentially it can impact our stress levels without us knowing, and it is an element that I refer to as *over-the-shoulder stress* – stress that seems to come from nowhere, but seemingly all of sudden and out of the blue, we feel overwhelmed and under-resourced to cope with a particular situation. Secondary trauma occurs when we feel stressed, anxious or distressed by hearing the traumatic account of a situation. This might be severe, such as the impact of witnessing the often relentless media accounts of local or worldwide tragedies such as the Black Saturday (or

any) bushfires, road trauma, storm damage or severe weather events. Our empathy for the immediate victims can become so significant that we find it difficult to leave these thoughts and we feel as though our consciousness is completely infiltrated. Proximity to such events, having visited the location, knowing people who live in the area or nearby are all potential elements that strengthen the emotional connection we feel for those who have been directly impacted. As an additional complication, we might also feel guilty for indulging our feelings to such an extent when we ourselves have not been directly affected, causing yet another layer of turmoil.

A different example of secondary trauma occurs when one hears many different, difficult stories, and is unable to find a release for the build-up of emotion. This is sometimes referred to as *compassion fatigue*, where individuals hear and/or support many people through their difficult stories and situations. Professions at risk here might include psychologists, counsellors, social workers, nurses, doctors and special education teachers, whose work is often based around assisting people with problems. Other industries exposed to difficult stories and/or potentially dangerous situations, often on a daily basis, might include finance workers, road workers, operational and non-operational emergency services staff, and welfare agency staff. This list is by no means exhaustive and, in reality, everyone is potentially exposed to secondary trauma; parents constantly assisting their children with daily hassles, children supporting ageing parents, colleagues assisting each other in the workplace, and of course managers, who are seeking the balance between performance and humanistic outcomes in the workplace.

The critical message here is that whilst it is clear that we are all exposed to many different forms of stress – some severe, some annoying, some temporary, and some longer-term – to manage stress effectively we need to firstly have awareness of ourselves, our personality, our response styles, and our thought processes, and secondly, our coping resources. We need to be aware of what outlets or supports are available to us, what works well for us and where the gaps are that we need to develop or strengthen.

We can choose how we think. Let's make it positive.

Merryn Snare

"If you are distressed by
anything external, the pain
is not due to the thing itself,
but to your estimate of it;
and this you have the power
to revoke at any moment."

Marcus Aurelius Antoninus

CHAPTER 2

Understanding Anxiety

What is anxiety?

Anxiety is a feeling of inner discomfort or turmoil that niggles and persists when one feels they are either in danger, or in a situation where they believe their coping resources are inadequate. It knows no boundaries and affects people across the entire socioeconomic spectrum and across all age groups. The causes of anxiety, although not fully understood, are varied and include personality traits, genetic predisposition, physical health issues, personal biochemistry and stressful life events[9,10]. Behaviour theories suggest anxiety disorders are learned and can therefore be unlearned, whilst the psychoanalytic view suggests anxiety stems from subconscious conflicts beginning in childhood[11].

Anxiety is difficult to specify. It is more internal than external and usually relates to vague feelings about things, such as a feeling that something bad is about to happen or a general sense of losing control. Whilst there are some situations where it would seem quite ‘normal’ to respond anxiously, it is important to determine the difference between what is normal and abnormal. This usually relates to the duration of the discomfort or anxiety, and the extent to which it impedes our daily functioning. For this reason, we must assess when our anxiety is no longer appropriate and more like an unwanted response to a situation. The vagueness of anxiety is one of its main points of difference from fear and phobia. Fear pertains to something concrete or specific and also within the realm of possibility, such as a fear of spiders, heights, needles, injections and the like, whilst phobias relate to an irrational fear about a specific or tangible ‘thing,’ unlike the obscurity of anxiety. Whilst anxiety is a common response affecting everyone at some stage to some degree, it is when it becomes debilitating or negatively impacts our daily functioning that we need to take stock and change our situation.

Essentially, anxiety links to the automatic part of our brain called the autonomic nervous system (ANS) which is responsible for the

involuntary functions of our body, such as breathing, coughing, salivation, perspiration or temperature control[12]. Within the ANS there are two streams; the sympathetic nervous system and the parasympathetic nervous system, which, although are often described as fulfilling opposing functions, are really functioning in a complementary manner. The sympathetic nervous system activates the 'fight or flight' response that bursts into action at the sense of danger, whilst the 'rest and digest' response of the parasympathetic nervous system assists in calming the nerves and recovery. When one perceives threat or danger, this automatic response unit (the sympathetic nervous system) swings into action, diverting blood flow from the gastrointestinal tract to the skeletal muscles and lungs, increasing heart rate, dilating pupils to enhance distance vision, and constricting intestinal and urinary functions. This is the body's preparation to fight off the danger or to flee from harm. This preparation also restricts the bodily functions that might slow us down, and it is the role of the parasympathetic nervous system to restore this balance once the threat has passed.

Anxiety might be considered a misfiring of this automatic response mechanism, since one frequently perceives danger that does not exist. The more we focus on the misfiring of our response systems, the more we overuse it, the less discerning we become towards what is really going on, and the more easily we indulge in anxious thinking. Given that anxiety is often described as a non-specific feeling of uneasiness or dread, a feeling that frequently has no specific cause or outcome because it is more a feeling of discomfort, it is important to understand one's thoughts and feelings that lead to such discomfort. Thoughts are particularly important as they are the chief driver of our perception and it is our perception of events or possible events that becomes the reality that determines our responses. Our feelings are also vital in anxiety management as these are often our first clue that our thinking is heading in a negative direction towards anxiety.

What are the symptoms of anxiety?

The fact that anxiety impacts our entire being all at once is why it is so uncomfortable.

Physiologically, we notice an increase in our heart rate, increased muscle tension, often a dry mouth, rapid breathing and increased sweating. Behaviourally it impedes our ability to act, express ourselves or deal with routine tasks, and psychologically we find ourselves in a subjective state of apprehension, uneasiness and detachment, often feeling that we have 'lost the plot', fearful of dying or going crazy.

Given that we all experience anxiety to some degree at some stage in our life, we need to learn to monitor our anxious responses to ensure that they do not inhibit our quality of life. We should see this as our 'need for change' notification.

The impacts of anxiety can be many and varied, ranging from a twinge of discomfort to a full-blown panic attack. A note of caution here: sometimes panic attack symptoms can mimic a serious health condition such as a heart attack. If you experience such symptoms you should always seek medical attention immediately for a full diagnosis. Once a physical problem is ruled out, you can then focus on dealing with the psychological situation.

The following list outlines some of the common symptoms of anxiety:

- Shortness of breath
- Heart palpitations
- Dizziness
- Trembling/shaking
- Feeling of choking
- Sweating
- Nausea/abdominal distress
- Feeling of unreality – as if you are 'not there'

- Numbness/tingling in hands or feet
- Hot and cold flashes
- Chest pain or discomfort
- Fear of going crazy or losing control
- Fear of dying
- Restlessness
- Poor sleep

Learning to manage these symptoms plays a critical role in managing anxiety.

What causes anxiety?

There are several contributing factors that lead to anxiety, including our genetic pre-disposition, personality and thinking styles, but perhaps the most notable of these pertains to thought processing – our belief systems and what we perceive as real. The list below outlines some of the most common factors contributing to anxiety, but this list is by no means exhaustive:

- Hereditary factors
- Biochemical factors
- Upbringing and family background
- Conditioning by parents, teachers, etc.
- Life experiences and recent stressors
- Personality styles and personal beliefs
- Thinking styles and self-talk
- Behavioural styles and the ability to express one's feelings

The Mind's Whiteboard

A common frustration for people struggling with anxiety is that they are often aware that their anxious thinking is irrational. This is particularly frustrating when they are also aware that most of the time they are very

rational and often high-functioning thinkers. It is the injection of creative thought that sets to work and brings us undone from a thought perspective.

Imagine your mind is like a whiteboard, and the salient points of your day are placed on there. When you are busy it is like the 'to do' list in your mind. Usually this works well for us but on occasion, when we are not actively engaged, our whiteboard seems empty, even though there is still plenty of space on it. We reportedly have between 50,000 and 70,000 thoughts per day, but an alarming percentage of these are 'junk thoughts' or 'faulty' thinking[13]. Usually we pay little or no attention to these junk thoughts, but at times, when we are not busy or are in a state of flux waiting for someone or something, instead of these 'junk thoughts' literally going in one ear and out of the other, an imaginary hook drops from the higher mind-space, catches a 'junk' thought and places it on our empty *mind's whiteboard*. There it is for us to see very clearly. It jumps out at us and provides us with something new to think about. Have you noticed how difficult it is to allow your mind some quiet time without it needing to find something to do? The next thing that happens is that with your natural creative ability, you consider this 'junk' thought and start questioning, "What if that is true? Maybe I should …? How should I …? What if…? What if …? What if …?" One doubting scenario leads to another and with each doubting or negative question we ask ourselves, we are adding more negativity, doubt, dread, fear and discomfort. In short, we are injecting creativity into our thinking and using it in a negative capacity, and before we know it, our whiteboard is full – not with a functional or fun-inspired 'to do' list, but with a single negative thought that we have made grow into an enormous drama which has infiltrated our perceived reality.

In essence, the more we focus on negative thoughts, the more life we give them. We need to accept and understand that anxious thinking is likely to affect all of us at some time – none of us are immune and our goal should be to recognise 'junk thoughts' for what they are and allow them to keep

The Mind's Whiteboard

THE MIND'S WHITEBOARD
Oh no! What if …
Maybe I should …
What if …… How will I cope!
This is dreadful, awful, shocking …
This is dreadful …

JUNK THOUGHT – you should have!!!

moving in one ear and out the other. If we learn to recognise that they are not real or rational, we can use stress reduction techniques to assist in letting go of anxiety as well as stress.

What is the impact of anxiety?

In addition to the discomfort resulting from anxiety, the impact disrupts daily living, further diminishing our quality of life. Disruption to sleep is a major impact, with many finding they are physically tired and ready for sleep but they are unable to stop their racing mind, or they wake feeling anxious and stressed and have difficulty falling back to sleep. Poor sleep can lead to a litany of issues, including difficulties in the workplace, creating a vicious cycle of further triggers for anxiety. The undermining of one's self-esteem is also prevalent with anxiety, leading to self-doubt and lower efficacy in many aspects of life, causing another downward spiral of negative thought. In severe cases, anxiety can co-exist with depression, which further compounds the disruptive and debilitating impact.

How is anxiety treated?

There are many anxiety disorders, some of which can have a severe impact and some of which can co-exist with other forms of anxiety or other mental health illnesses. These include Social Anxiety, Panic Attack, Generalised Anxiety Disorder (GAD), Post Traumatic Stress Disorder (PTSD) and Obsessive Compulsive Disorder (OCD) to name a few. Of these I will make brief mention of Panic Attacks, as these are relatively common and are usually perpetuated by faulty thinking; the fear of having another attack. Panic attacks are spontaneous – they are not necessarily triggered by situations or places, but tend to occur out of the blue, and can even happen when the person is relaxed. They often have strong physiological symptoms, which can mimic a heart attack, and in these cases it is important to visit your doctor for a correct diagnosis. Typically, the symptoms of a panic attack come first and the panic occurs in response to the symptoms, which becomes a continuing cycle that perpetuates panic

attacks. Panic Disorder is the fear of having a spontaneous panic attack and is usually diagnosed when an individual has experienced at least two spontaneous panic attacks followed by one month of persistent concern of having another. Ironically, it is this persistent concern that causes much of one's distress and also makes one more vulnerable to having another attack. Hence, recovery requires losing the fear of having an attack, which also requires letting go of the need to be in control. This illustrates the critical role our thinking plays in recovery from anxiety issues and to this end the role of our emotions comes to the fore. If we consider that there are two types of thought – rational and irrational – it is usually the emotional interplay that separates these. When we use negative emotions in our thinking, our usual rationality becomes overwhelmed and instead turns to irrational thinking. We need, therefore, to apply positive emotions to our thoughts in order to enhance our self-belief and support rationality, rather than wind ourselves down with negatively-laden irrational views. In these cases it is wise to consult your doctor or mental health practitioner for assistance.

Given the far-reaching impact of anxiety, it is essential that intervention caters for all levels of impact – physiological, behavioural and psychological. This requires a diminishing of the physiological symptoms, assisting and enhancing the behavioural outcomes (such as eliminating avoidance), and changing or reframing subjective self-talk which feeds apprehension. The traits that perpetuate anxiety include perfectionism, an excessive need for approval, ignoring the physical and psychological symptoms of stress, and an excessive need for control. This highlights the need to understand and modify one's thought processing to effectively manage anxiety.

CBT is an evidence-based treatment, which is generally considered the treatment of choice for anxiety disorders[5,11]. CBT includes relaxation, breathing techniques, exposure to places and situations one has been avoiding, and thought-based techniques, with the aim being to change

fearful interpretations of the symptoms, and thus break the anxiety-producing thoughts. Whilst CBT is a useful therapy, the individual must be committed to doing the work – it doesn't happen by osmosis!

For the purposes of this book, my focus is on the milder forms of anxiety where, as with stress, a level of self-awareness and simple and effective strategies can be adopted to experience relief. At this level, you should then be able to monitor your thoughts, feelings and behaviours, enabling you to annihilate stress and anxiety before they takeover. I will discuss some of the elements of CBT as strategies you can implement and will also outline how you can learn to heighten your awareness of changes in your mind-state before full blown stress and/or anxiety takes over.

Be aware of what you allow
on your mind's whiteboard.

Merryn Snare

If you want your life to be more rewarding, you have to change the way you think.

Oprah Winfrey

CHAPTER 3

Understanding our Thought Patterns

Thoughts and Thinking

Recently I was fortunate enough to travel to Fiji to visit my daughter who is working in Suva. I took the local bus from Nadi to Suva and a delightful Fijian lady named Veronica sat next to me. We struck up a conversation and after taking a call on her mobile phone she showed me a photo of her daughter, a lovely vibrant looking young girl who appeared younger than her 32 years. She had been working in Suva before moving to India to undertake further studies. The lady then said, "She passed away three weeks ago." Naturally, I was taken aback by this, and we talked a bit about loss, how she was feeling and how she was managing her grief. Fijians are deeply religious and this was clearly a tremendous support for her but after a while she said, "You know, I am very grateful that she didn't have to live wheelchair-bound and that she didn't experience all of the dreadful things her doctors had expected."

Despite this tragic loss of a young life, Veronica was able to see some relative positives in the situation. This does not mean that this mother was not heart-broken, grieving and hurting deeply. However, it does illustrate how her ability to see positives in a tragically sad situation was assisting her to manage on a day-to-day level. She was certainly open to the love and support offered to her by the community and she was able to talk about how she felt – she was not denying her feelings. In essence, Veronica's *belief systems* enabled her to find the relative positives, which assisted her in finding peace within a tragic and personally devastating situation.

It is interesting to note that in the majority of cases, it is the negative life events from which we learn the most, and from which we experience the greatest amount of personal growth. It seems that when things are going well, we lap up the fun and enjoy the good times, almost taking them for granted. We rarely acknowledge or express our appreciation for the good things in life but when things go badly, we hurt and the pain forces us to take note of what has happened, what has gone wrong and how things are different from the times when we blithely cruised

along on easy street. The pain makes us sit up and take notice of what we now know we definitely do not like! As we set about rectifying the contributing factors to our pain, we learn along the way what we need to change about how we have been living or existing.

As human beings, we are privileged to possess that highly sophisticated organ called the brain and its equally amazing capacity called the mind, which generates a host of cognitive functions including thought, perception, emotion and memory. As individuals, we all have our own unique blend of cognitive functioning, which, as mentioned earlier, is influenced by hereditary factors, personality styles and environmental factors. What is clear is the fact that our thinking, perception or interpretation of events has a major influence on how we experience the outcome of such events. The good news is that we can learn to change our thinking, and by learning to adapt to our circumstances and environment, we can have a significant impact on our personal stress levels, which translates to our levels of balance and happiness.

Broadly speaking, as with stress, there are two types of thinking – positive and negative. In the arena of stress and anxiety, there is considerable focus on negative thoughts, which tend to form a basis or springboard from which stress and anxiety can launch. If you consider your thinking style in the context of the 'glass half full' versus the 'glass half empty', you may make an assessment as to where you fit. I think of this as the *glass of optimism*. Which are you – a 'glass half full' person, who is optimistic and always finds the positive side, or a 'glass half empty' person, whose thoughts and rhetoric reflect pessimism and fear? You might also wonder what makes you lean to one or the other. What is it that makes people differ so dramatically in their thinking style? Is it a genetic predisposition? Does it result from the environment in which one grew up and the role modeling one was exposed to, or is it a result of life circumstances and experiences? How can family members be so different in their thinking styles?

The nature versus nurture debate frequently surrounds these questions, and given the complexity of the human being, the brain and our intricate cognitions or thought patterns, it is the uniqueness and individuality of psychology that makes human behaviour so fascinating. An obvious starting point is to consider the role models provided by our parents; their thought processes and behavioural traits. Were they positive people, or did they tend to defer to negativity, have a doomsday view, or were they driven by fear? On a somewhat different plane, but still within the same gene pool and similar environmental setting, are our siblings. How do we compare with their thought patterns? How similar or different are they to us and why? The fact that our siblings can be very different from ourselves might make us question whether genetic predisposition counts for much, a lot, or whether it is all just about one's unique personality traits.

With regard to the influence of familial role modeling, it is important to consider the socioeconomic and generational times of parents or significant others compared with ourselves. This is often referred to as the 'generation gap', which tends to conjure up images of 'fuddy duddy' conservatism, but in reality it is a significant and very real influence on the development of each generation. It relates to the era of each generation economically, technologically and politically. For example, the parents of Baby Boomers lived through the World Wars and, depending upon the country in which they lived, the impact of this was variable but arguably significant across most of the globe. Following the Wars was the Great Depression, which instilled fear into most who lived through it, even if they were not directly impacted. It seemed that everyone knew someone who had lost their job or their house or could not afford food, and everyone was subjected to the rationing of food and other goods like building materials, which were crucial in kick-starting economic recovery. Whilst it would be naïve to think these problems do not exist today, it was the broad scale of the impact of the Depression that seemed to create fear in the minds of many, which probably lead to a

generation or two of individuals who developed more negativity in their thinking as individuals, and subsequently as parents and role models, than other generations. As a tail-end Baby Boomer myself, I notice, on reflection, that my mother in particular, was very concerned about the impact of the Depression, not on herself specifically, but on what she had seen with people around her, and I believe much of her thinking was influenced by her role models who were trying to raise, protect and provide for their family. As the youngest of a fairly large family she was also exposed to people who were scarred by the war and very scared for the future, which I believe impacted her life experience and shaped her thinking. The up side of the Depression was that people learned to be very practical, to which there was none better than my father. To my mind, he could make, fix or do anything. He threw nothing away, and I have vivid memories of his workshop, which was testament to his thriftiness. Amongst his many treasures he had a jar of the tiniest stubs of lead pencils, so small that you could barely hold them, sharpened to a fine point for marking his timber creations. A cabinet maker by trade, he also built our family home – literally. He carted water from a local billabong to mix the mortar for the brickwork. Given that building materials were difficult to come by as a result of the depression, he saved anything he thought he might find a use for, and all the 'good stuff' was stored in the garage, shed, workshop and under the house ready for a potential future need. When he decided to add a rumpus room to our house, he remembered he had a large pane of glass stored under the house. It had been there for 25 years, waiting for that perfect opportunity to be used. As he carefully measured the pane and the opening, and built the window frame to suit, the big day for installation arrived. After carefully installing this large sheet of glass, he stepped back to admire his handiwork, only to notice a small crack had appeared!

In addition to these fear factors of war and economic depression, there is also the influence of technology and I venture to suggest that apart from the Wars and the Great Depression, technological advancements

have made the biggest impact on society as we know it today. My grandmother saw the invention of the motorcar and my parents were fortunate to own a car and they both drove. It was fairly uncommon for women to drive when I was young, and many families did not have things like cars, televisions, or even telephones. How would Generation X and Y manage to survive?!When I reached driving age I was one of the fortunate few who managed to save up to buy my own car straight away, and as technology advanced, we soon saw two cars in most adult Baby Boomer households. Now we see a car for every adult in the household, a landline telephone in most rooms of every house, plus at least one mobile phone for every person from primary school age up – or so it seems. In fact it is becoming increasingly common to see householders abandoning landlines in favour of mobile phones, which have become a more economical means of telecommunication. I have even met mothers who call their young children in from play by using their mobile phones! Of course, computers didn't really start to reach our homes until some of the Gen Xs were children, let alone the range of devices we have to choose from today, such as PCs, laptops, tablets and smart phones. Many people, including non-tech savvy Baby Boomers like me, have at least one of each!

The advancement in technology has emerged well beyond the home and the area of medical science is where we all applaud and potentially benefit from these amazing discoveries. I frequently notice significant differences in the thinking styles of Baby Boomers or their parents compared with Generations X or Y. For some Baby Boomers the childhood memories of the seemingly barbaric treatment methods used in medical or dental procedures remain vivid. It is not uncommon for me to counsel Baby Boomers who have not been to the dentist in years as they are too fearful. Fearful of what? Pain? "Yes, but no, not really… actually I am not really sure why," is a common response I hear. There is an array of answers, which are not really definitive, but what is clear for them is that there is some form of discomfort that has been significant

enough to prevent them from seeking regular checkups. Even though there is now a range of procedures designed to minimise pain, many are still haunted by the memories of their early experiences, which is testament to my earlier comment about the strength of the impact of events we perceive as negative. However, this fear is not rational. It is based on emotions that occurred in the past, possibly fuelled by well-meaning adults, whose personal experiences may also have deemed a trip to the dentist as terrifying. This further highlights the influence our role models can have on establishing and reinforcing our *belief structures*, and if we as role models are not aware of our behaviours and how we project our thoughts, we will be role modelling our fears to our children. Hence, the importance of overcoming our fears becomes crystal clear. In addition to improving our personal quality of life, it also protects against modeling irrational fear-related behaviour to our children.

Take a few moments now to ponder the familial impact on your own being.

A word of caution here – we are not trying to rid ourselves of all fear. There are times when it is prudent to have some fear and to take precautions around that. For example, a lady rang me and asked me to assist her daughter to let go of her fear of tiger snakes. This teenager was part of a school rowing team and on one occasion they went to their sculls to find a tiger snake curled up inside. This occurred only a short time after the teenager had experienced an earlier encounter with a tiger snake, where she and a friend had been in a canoe on the same river and the snake had chased them across the river, rearing up in preparation to strike. The fact that these encounters both occurred in the spring, when the weather was becoming warmer and snakes will fiercely defend their nests and territories, illustrates the wisdom of holding an astute awareness in one's native environment. In this situation, the fact that snakes are about at this particular time of year and that they like to sun themselves or curl up in warm places where they won't be disturbed, together with maintaining a very healthy respect of these venomous

creatures, is crucial. I do not see this as an irrational fear and vigilance for rowers and all boat enthusiasts in these environments is essential.

Having outlined the impact our upbringing can have on our thought patterns, I would now like to direct the focus to the broad categories of thinking – positive and negative – and the role our negative thinking style has on stress and anxiety. Negative self-talk is an internal monologue that is automatic and subtle – in fact we are often unaware of it. It is frequently a telegraphic or clipped version of speech or single-word thoughts or related images that lead to a series of irrational thoughts which we manage to make sound credible. The give-away words include, "what if?" which anticipates the worst before it happens or, "if only" which sets up ruminations that can only spiral downwards. This scare talk (e.g. "*what if* I have a heart attack?") commandeers the physiological system and before you know it, can lead to full blown panic. There are different forms of negative self-talk; the worrier who increases anxiety, the critic who decimates their self-esteem, the victim who promotes depression, and the perfectionist who is never satisfied with their efforts, leading to chronic stress and burnout.

I picture negative thinking as a spring that goes on and on and on, spiralling continuously, and usually in a downwards direction. Unless you manage to cut that spring or stop it, one negative thought leads to another until they all connect with each other, creating a huge pity party that builds into an overwhelming mass of 'headspin' or confusion that becomes bigger than Ben-Hur. As negative thoughts spiral downward on this spring, they appear to develop an eternal life unless we take charge of our thinking and do something about it.

The diagram opposite illustrates the impact of *energetic dehydration* on the *glass of optimism*. Whether you start with your glass 'half full' or 'half empty', the spiraling negative thoughts will ensure that it soon becomes completely empty, sapping your emotional energy to the point of *energetic dehydration*.

Energetic Dehydration

Draining the Glass of Optimism

Negative thoughts spiral down, sapping your energy along the way

It can seem like a bottomless glass

The really important message here is that you can change your thought patterns – isn't that great news? If you are a negative thinker, if you have had negative thinking role models, or if you have had negativity as your default setting when something difficult has occurred in the past, you can actually change that and learn how to look for the positive, finding the opportunity within the challenge. This is a really fantastic gift and it is available to everyone. This does not mean that you should have some perverse kind of celebration when trouble strikes, but rather it is more about managing your reactions which will free up your emotional resources to better equip you for dealing with problems.

It seems to have taken me time to learn this, but now when something doesn't go the way I thought it should have, or more to the point, the way I would have liked it to, I am very comfortable in asking myself, "What am I meant to be learning from this?" Whilst my purpose in the first instance is to find an opportunity and a challenge from the disappointment, at the very least I am learning something, usually a valuable lesson that I could not see at the time, and highlighting what I would do differently next time. It is important to acknowledge that no one is perfect. We are not going to do things perfectly all of the time and we will not get things right all of the time. Many of us pay lip service to this sentiment but for all of the perfectionists out there, it is time to ease up on your expectations. One of the greatest ways of learning is through our mistakes, and if we give ourselves the grace and the space to be able to look at what we might have done differently or how we might have done it better, we are making an important contribution to the process of shifting our thinking patterns and thought processes from where we are currently functioning.

An example that I like to use to illustrate the importance of learning from mistakes is the process of learning how to tie shoelaces. I know in the days of Velcro shoe fasteners some children might never learn this skill, however, I believe it is a really important fine motor skill as most

people will need to tie shoelaces at some stage. If you think about the trial and error involved in getting the loops the right size and then pulling them tight enough so the shoes stay done up, it is quite a challenge. It's only by repeating this process and doing it over and over, making small modifications to get it right, that the task is mastered.

Some people refer to this as *failing forward* but if you find the word 'failing' has negative connotations (which will stem from the founding belief system you accepted as a young child) then label it differently – *learning from experience* perhaps. The essence of the lesson is that we learn from mistakes and as long as we take something beneficial from the experience, it has not been a waste.

This highlights the importance of self-esteem and healthy thought processes. Self-esteem encompasses a way of thinking, feeling and acting that suggests you accept, respect, trust and believe in yourself. Acceptance requires that you are comfortable with your strengths and weaknesses and that you do not expect perfection (by the standards of your early formed beliefs) in everything you do.

Respect suggests the acknowledgment of your dignity, the valuing of yourself and treating yourself as you would another whom you respect, whilst trust and belief in yourself is reflected in consistency in your behaviour and feelings which provide a sense of stability, regardless of the external world. Without these elements, low self-esteem leaves one feeling empty and makes it difficult to address or reframe their thought processes, which enable healthy functioning.

Unhelpful Thinking Styles

Black-and-White Thinking

Our beliefs have a profound impact on how we view the world and how we interpret the behaviour, actions and communication of others. One of the factors that I find contributes significantly to an individual's tendency

towards 'black-and-white thinking' is the importance of being 'right.' As I reflect on my teaching experience, particularly my years of working with young children, as well as my own development and that of my daughter, it seems that we have an inherent need to be seen to be 'good.' We are taught both at home and school that behaving well equates to being 'good' and the only alternative to this is being naughty, getting into trouble, or being seen as 'bad'. This style of thinking has developed as a result of our *belief structures*, which were modelled to us as children. These belief frameworks were role modelled by our parents and significant others – the very people who we believed to always be right – and were the only responses that we knew of as we were learning and developing the skills of thought and meaning. We had no other benchmarks or the ability to think critically at this stage in our development. Our sense of self and self-esteem are inextricably linked to this notion of being 'good' and being 'good' seems to equate with being 'right.' To compound this confusing notion even further, it is getting things 'right' at school that attracts praise. Getting things 'wrong' is a sure signal that we didn't try hard enough, we were careless or just didn't have the smarts.

Different ≠ Wrong

Consequently, the notion of right and wrong often becomes well entrenched in our need to win arguments or to badger the point until the other person backs down and, of course, if and when this doesn't happen (often because our fellow communicator has developed a similar need to be right), we tend to leave such discussions feeling unheard, unappreciated, and with our self-esteem a little battered. The other unfortunate consequence of this scenario is that too often the best of both points of view can be missed, all in the name of someone needing to be 'right'. So, my message here is quite simply that *different does not equal wrong*. There is bound to be merit in what both parties have to say and needing to win the contest usually leaves the situation outcome coming up short.

Emotional Interpretations

Another important element that influences our thinking and our responses is our perception of what is going on around us. It is often said that our perception is our reality and whilst this is true, I am going to assist you in training your brain to put some additional steps into the personal perception of reality dynamic.

Always consider the *two pairs of shoes*

The first of these is the key point that everyone sees things differently. We each have our own perspective on everything and that's why we may well react differently to things and others around us. This links to the ABC model I mentioned earlier, where the beliefs of the individual determine their response to a particular stimulus. A quick and fun exercise that illustrates this is to ask two people sitting in the same room to tell you what they can see. It is interesting to see who notices what the similarities and differences are. The really important point about this notion is what I refer to as the *two pairs of shoes* – yours and theirs. If you are annoyed, upset or maybe even hurt by the comments or position of another, before you take it too personally say to yourself, "I wonder what they meant." Also try to imagine the situation from their perspective – does it make a little more sense now? Can you understand why they may have said or done what they did, even if it is not your reality? At the very least, are you able to take the affront a little less personally? Clarification is an extremely important part of communication and we often find that had we clarified things when they first happened, we could have saved ourselves much grief and heartache.

A particularly important example of this approach relates to our emotions, especially anger. Imagine a friend has 'bumped' you from a social engagement at the last minute. You have both had this in your diary for ages and you were really looking forward to it. With no real explanation,

your friend calls at the last minute to say they can't make it. How do you feel? Let down? Concerned? Annoyed? Hurt? Frustrated? Angry? With no real explanation it is difficult to know what is going on with your friend. Has a crisis occurred? If so, why wouldn't they tell you? Under such circumstances you would fully understand and be there to assist. Are they upset with you for something you have no idea about, or have they just found other more important things to do? But what, you might ask, could be more important than your friendship?

Clearly, the best solution to such a situation is to clarify with your friend what is happening. I should point out that such behaviour in itself may indicate that your friend has some psychological issues that are new to them, that they are possibly unable to define or express, or may even be unaware of. Withdrawing from social contact is a common symptom of depression, and friends and colleagues often notice such symptoms before the person is aware of or able to acknowledge them.

This explanation alone is already moving the focus away from the original act that triggered your negative emotions. What is important from your perspective in response to feeling let down or dumped by your friend is the fact that you have moved the focus away from your own feelings of negativity fairly quickly. This process is not about denying how you feel, but rather acknowledging how these episodes made you feel and the emotions that came into play (and you will notice that these were probably all negative emotions). It is an essential part of your self-awareness and you should use this life experience to help you better understand yourself and others. To move forward from this experience and to assist in mitigating change via your thought patterns, it is important not to dwell on the negative emotions. Notice them, but then consider what might have been happening for your friend that you are unaware of – think about their (*the other*) *pair of shoes*. This can be of great assistance when you are formulating some discussion points to raise with your friend at a later stage. For example, although you may have been really upset and

annoyed at the time, acknowledging the *two pairs of shoes* allows you some breathing space before confronting your friend and possibly saying something you might later regret. You may then ask something like "Is everything all right?" The type of response you receive will give you an indication as to where things are at with your friend.

The emotion of anger is one that requires special attention, as we know from research that anger is linked to health hazards including cardiac issues[14]. Whilst the Type A personality is usually more prone to anger responses than the laid-back Type B personality, the state of anger can be lingering and enduring if we allow it[15]. The key point to keep in mind when you are angry is that whatever someone has done to leave you feeling angry, in most situations they are either unaware of the state they have caused you or they have moved on. What this means is that you are left holding the anger. It is all yours. And basically, who wants it? The person who has caused your anger has moved on and you need to deal with the anger to enable you to do the same. Easier said than done? Definitely. But also do-able.

If you find yourself feeling angry, first of all it is important to understand who or what has made you angry. Ask yourself why you are feeling this way and also ask yourself to consider the *other pair of shoes*. What might have been going on for them? Did they really mean it the way you have perceived it? Might there have been a different intention?

Intention versus Perception

Intention versus perception is perhaps one of the most common elements of miscommunication. This occurs when someone has said something with an intended message but may receive an unexpected response. If we think about our notion of the *two pairs of shoes*, the other person involved in the exchange may perceive the comment in a very different way from how it was intended. This does not have to be a blame game, as

it might simply be a miscommunication or a misunderstanding. As you become more aware of your thought processes, you will have the ability to recognise your feelings of frustration and before allowing them to flow into a river of distress, you will be able to clarify the communication. In other words, check what was really meant before you react– it may save you considerable grief! This is not to say that there won't be times when you feel justifiably upset and angry with someone, but when this happens, the best approach is to acknowledge what and how you are feeling, then examine what you might be able to do to improve the situation, and once you have a plan in mind, adopt some of the stress release techniques that we will discuss later in this book to assist in managing your distress.

Catastrophic Thinking

This thinking style is typified by individuals defaulting to the worst-case scenario when difficult, uncomfortable, or situations perceived to be outside of their control, arise. Common amongst 'glass half empty' people who tend towards pessimism, catastrophic thinkers ruminate about irrational outcomes, succumbing to their fears and negative belief systems. They usually lack the self-belief in their coping abilities or the clarity of what is a reasonable expectation for the given circumstances. The thoughts of catastrophic thinkers race from one dire possibility to another and they are, of course, certain that their catastrophic predictions will eventuate. Take the example of a woman who works in a restaurant and is on the evening shift. Her partner is at home and is aware that her finishing times can vary but tonight is cold, wet and windy, and conditions on the roads are hazardous. Normally her partner would be relaxed and would often go to bed before she came home. However, tonight he cannot settle. He is concerned that she has been in a car accident, even although it is unlikely that she would have finished work by now. He has tried to call her mobile even although he knows she won't pick up if she is working. He contemplates ringing the local hospitals to see if his partner has been taken to the emergency department. In reality, when we stop to think about the range of possible outcomes, we can see that there

are usually several possibilities. In this example of the restaurant worker, apart from the fact that it is unusual for her to finish early, the cold, wet weather usually attracts more diners to the restaurant as it has a warm and inviting open fire. The staff also have a meal when the patrons have left and then there is the clean up after a busy night. This highlights some of the possibilities other than the imagined catastrophe, and is part of the CBT approach that is helpful for catastrophic thinkers, who need to learn how to manage their thinking to enable them to elicit rational thought, thereby reducing their stress responses.

So, we can see that there are several unhelpful thinking styles that needlessly lead to increased stress and anxiety. The first step in annihilating this stress and anxiety is to be aware of our thinking style and *belief structures* in order to provide the basis for positive change. And remember, change is very do-able.

> **There are many ways of achieving a suitable outcome. Different does not equal wrong.**
>
> **Merryn Snare**

Part 2

LEARNING TO CHANGE YOUR MIND

Happiness depends
upon ourselves.

Aristotle

Part 2

LEARNING TO CHANGE YOUR MIND

> Happiness depends upon ourselves.
>
> **Aristotle**

CHAPTER 4

Who is in Charge?

Who is in charge? You are, of course. *You* are in charge of your life. You can change your thinking, your beliefs and your responses to stress. You can learn to be more positive in your thinking and find the opportunity in challenge, which is great news. And since we really are in charge, our next step is to learn how to make great choices and decisions that serve us well.

It is important to remember that we all have a choice. Even although there may be times when you lament that you 'have no choice,' this is usually because you believe that none of the options available to you are desirable. In conjunction with what you now understand about thought processes, the task becomes more about filtering your old expectations as well as the expectations of others and focusing on what you believe is right. Whilst there is always, of course, an unwritten assumption that your behaviour will operate within the laws of the land, it is now time to check in with your personal values, morals and ethics. Look at what *you* believe in and how that manifests in your daily behaviour and self-expectation. Understand that although you might be keen to please those near and dear to you, you need to ensure that in seeking such approval you are first pleasing to and approving of yourself. Allow your inner being or your intuition to be your guide. Once you have learned to trust your own views and given yourself permission for your opinions to be your own, rather than needing them to match or be approved of by family, friends, managers or influential others, you are now ready to work on changing your responses. This involves digging deeply into your mind to fathom what your negative beliefs have been based on, whether they still make sense to you, and then setting about modifying those beliefs that were obstructing your mind's freedom and preventing you from being you.

At this point it is pertinent to mention the role of fear, which frequently plays a significant role in people's emotions, and often stems from the mindset they developed during childhood. Reflecting on the earlier chapters and comments about the generation of one's parents,

fear – particularly around scarcity – has had a major contribution to the thinking of many. Referring to the earlier example of the generation who lived during the years of the World Wars and the Depression, it would seem that this fear was modelled and transferred to the mindset of many Baby Boomers. Children who were raised in the 1940s and 1950s were taught to conserve everything and not waste precious resources, especially food. This stringent conservation of resources emerged through a fear of lack, rather than the more current-day thinking of living sustainably. Similarly, it would not be unexpected if the impact of war or devastation impacted the thinking styles of people in other parts of the world at various times throughout history; Vietnam, Bosnia, the Middle East, the Falkland Islands, to mention just a few regions that have experienced significant challenges, and we might expect the impact of living under these circumstances to be passed from one generation to the next. It is important to understand these significant influences. It is not about judging. However, for each individual, the first step is about understanding the platform of their role models, whilst the second step is about deciding which old habits, beliefs and thinking styles one would happily discard before setting about reinventing a thinking style that serves you better.

Acknowledging the influences and impact of your upbringing is important, but from here my challenge to you is to not let that stop you from taking charge of your thinking and change that which no longer serves you. Now you are living in your own unique and different time and space. As an adult, you are living in a world that is different from that of your childhood. You have your own thought power and you can alter or minimise the clouds of stress and anxiety to a large extent, via your thought choices. Once we understand how and why our fearful thinking has emerged, we are well placed to understand the acronym for fear; False Evidence Appearing Real. Take some time to identify and understand exactly what your fears are and whether or not there is any substance to it. If there is good reason for fear, examine what you

need to assist in managing that fear. Is it resources, education, work or professional expertise? Or something else?

Exposure Therapy

From a clinical perspective there are many of ways of dealing with fear. A well-known strategy is exposure therapy, where an individual, under the guidance of their therapist, is exposed to gradually increasing amounts or intensity of the situation or 'thing' that is the root cause of their fear[16]. This approach is often used for phobias although, in my view, should not be attempted until the client is fully prepared for that step. In my work with arachnophobia, I have found many clients are extremely anxious about unexpected exposure. They are concerned that despite my assurances that I will not be springing any surprise spiders on them as part of the treatment, I will do so anyway, and for some clients this has happened (not by me!). Apart from being irresponsible, this strategy of power and control by the clinician helps no one. The clients usually end up more fearful than when they started and the clinician damages their reputation.

To highlight the importance of ensuring the process of exposure therapy follows the client's needs, I will outline the journey a client and I embarked on following an extremely difficult workplace event. A client was falsely accused of making threatening phone calls and the accusers had absolutely no evidence but tried to scare and bully the client into admitting to something they had not done. Eventually it became clear to the workplace that not only was their internal intelligence false but they had also caused significant trauma to one of their loyal and dedicated staff. This client was understandably extremely traumatised by this event, but possessed the personal strength and resolve to work at overcoming the resulting psychological damage. Working initially with the immediate aspects of the trauma, the client's condition improved significantly in the short term. However, over time it was evident that there were elements of PTSD that needed attention. We worked on and

off over a five-year period, leaving time to consolidate the steps taken and goals achieved. My intention for this client was to return to the pre-trauma condition with regard to comfort, calmness, personal security and the ability to live life to the full. I was also aware that this client was likely to experience significant personal growth as a part of this process, which would lead them to even greater levels of self-esteem and self-awareness than they had previously known.

The final part of my work with this client required exposure to the location where the episode occurred but it is important to point out that it took several years following the episode for the client to be ready and psychologically strong enough to take this step. This was an essential part of the treatment as the client had been avoiding this location, even though it was within their local community, and avoidance was impeding the quality of life not only for the client but also for their entire family. We took the exposure to the location very gently, building up the degree of difficulty of the task in alignment with what the client thought they could manage. After five years, this client returned to a place of feeling comfortable enough to live, work and socialise within the community without feeling impeded by the psychological dread that resulted from the workplace episode. I should reiterate that it was the client's willingness to work through the challenges over time that was key to their success.

This case highlights the significant impact that traumatic experiences can have on many aspects of one's life and how a willingness to work at dealing with all symptoms, even if it is years after the event, is critical to a successful outcome and a positive quality of life.

Reframing Thoughts

Another less intense strategy that I find works well in managing fear is to translate the concept of fear into a new perspective. If you think about fear as clouds and then ask yourself what a white, fluffy cloud contains, the answer is water. White fluffy clouds look innocuous and might be

described as beautiful, soft or delicate. If you then think of a big, thick, black cloud, it somehow appears much more ominous and threatening, but, it also contains water. What is it about these two sets of descriptors that altered your visual interpretation of clouds? It is your perception. We have learned to associate black clouds with a sense of danger or as a warning for rugged weather ahead, even if in fact the storm blows over without so much as a drop of rain falling. If one relates this thought process to fear, what we may initially perceive as a foreboding situation, when breaking it down and looking closely at what our fear is about, we frequently find that it is not as dire as we initially thought. This fear, which has been preoccupying and wasting way too much of our emotional and thought energy, has created or reinforced a negative outlook and a negative approach, which need to be changed. This is often referred to as *reframing* our thoughts.

How one approaches fear, links to one's self-awareness, mindset and thinking patterns. More importantly, being aware of the potential for fear to represent *false evidence appearing real* challenges our mindset, providing an opportunity to change or improve our thought patterns, and ultimately, to live more freely. Pitching self-expectations at a reasonable level, allowing yourself the time and space to learn from mistakes and accepting your best efforts, will have a huge impact on your ability to learn and understand who you are, how your thinking influences your quality of life, and what you might choose to alter to assist in establishing the balanced life you deserve.

Time to Live Better

For me, the notion of living better is about balance and harmony. These states are absolutely essential, particularly if we are going to manage stress and anxiety and still enjoy a great quality of life. It is important to understand that stress and anxiety are normal, common and natural phenomena – they exist and are going to affect us all at some time.

Stress is a normal, everyday occurrence and we cannot, nor should we, try to prevent it. What is important, however, is that we monitor and manage our awareness of the build-up of stress and our response to it. We need a similar approach to anxiety with an understanding of the origins of our anxious thoughts, together with an awareness of the cues that can operate as our early warning system.

Balance and harmony are vital elements in maintaining sound mental health and wellbeing, and it is no accident that as I am working on this book, I am actually in Fiji having a break. Yes, working during a break may seem questionable but it can also be inspiring. Relaxing whilst on holiday, in a beautiful location surrounded by beautiful people is ideal for unwinding, whilst also making it possible for me to think clearly and calmly and find time to focus on my long-held goal, which would be difficult to fit into my daily life at home. For these reasons, I decided to combine the best of both worlds. I believe holidays, breaks and occasional indulgences are an essential element of balance and harmony, although that does not necessarily mean going to Fiji or some other tropical paradise. It might mean having a weekend off to be with family and friends, camping in the bush or perhaps a day off having lunch with a friend. It might also mean treating yourself to a massage or going to a sporting event. There are many ways that you can enjoy a break and recharge your batteries.

The most important thing is to DO IT.
Make sure that you prioritize and get around to doing it.

There are different types of balance, and you have probably heard and read much about work-life balance, which seems to be increasingly difficult to maintain. It also seems that regular working hours, whatever they may be these days, now seem inadequate to cover what appears to be ever-increasing workloads. I frequently talk to many people who believe

that they don't have time to take their lunch breaks or their tea breaks because they are so snowed under with work, they want to make a great impression on their manager, or whatever their reason might be. This issue has been highlighted in research that suggests many Australians are missing their lunch and tea breaks largely due to time pressures[17]. However the knock-on effects of this is that they grab unhealthy snacks and develop poor eating habits, as well as suffering increased levels of fatigue and lowered energy, particularly in that afternoon siesta time, which all defeats the purpose of fitting more into their working day. The other side of the story however, is that some employers are mindful of work-life balance and encourage their staff to take their breaks. In fact, I think many workplaces would be horrified if they realised people were not taking their breaks, and yet, it still happens. What are workplaces missing? It is definitely to the workplace's advantage that people maintain a work-life balance, as this leads to greater productivity and efficiency by means of a fresher, happier and more reliable workforce, which translates to a more profitable bottom line.

Mind-body balance is also crucial for wellbeing and it is common for people to find that their body may be fatigued and ready to rest, whilst their mind is still racing. This is a common element in disruptive sleep patterns and an effective way of managing this imbalance is to ensure that you maintain regular physical exercise. It might be tempting to use the excuse that you are too tired to exercise, but exercise is exactly what you need. It is important to have a medical checkup with your doctor before embarking on any new exercise regime, and you should exercise within your capability, but just like that famous tick says; "just do it".

The culmination of balance becomes what I refer to as *whole life balance*. Work, rest, play, eat, drink, socialize, exercise – everything in appropriate proportions will set a sound platform for happiness and wellbeing.

You are in charge of your life.
Make it count.

Merryn Snare

Happiness is not the absence
of problems, but the ability
to deal with them.

Charles de Montesquieu

CHAPTER 5

21 Stress Strategies PART 1

Strategies for Immediate Relief

Now that you have greater clarity around your unique thinking and behavioural style, and your responses to and the potential build-up of stress and anxiety, I now want to share the strategies that I refer to as the *PEARLS* with you. I have found that these are not only helpful but essential in assisting clients (and myself) in creating personal balance and harmony. These *PEARLS* are divided into four groups, each group having a different application, and whilst all are important in enabling you to establish balance and harmony in your personal world, I encourage you to review each strategy and select the strategies that best suit *you.* Learn how to integrate them into your being and use them! They will not help at all if you keep them in your kitbag and never bring them out.

Some of the *PEARLS* will be simple to adopt. Others will require more effort. It is really about understanding all of them, adding them to your toolkit and knowing that you can draw on the most appropriate strategy in a given situation whenever you need or choose to. It is important that you have an inner awareness and confidence in the fact that you possess a range of strategies that you can use to help you manage your stress and anxiety. It is a mindset 'thing'. Simply knowing that you have the tools to use is extremely useful in assisting with managing stress and anxiety, as one of the most challenging elements of stress and anxiety is that feeling of being overwhelmed. When you are overwhelmed, it is very difficult to believe that you can be in control of anything. If you reflect on all of the previous discussion, this entire book is about you learning to have more control of you. Your mindset needs to be one of "I can manage this. I will be able to cope."

As we head into the next chapters, we will be looking at my 21 *PEARLS*; the tools and strategies that I have found to be the most useful to clients in my clinical practice, and I will outline how you might use them and what they might offer.

STRATEGY 1 STOP

This is an extremely powerful *thought stopping* technique. The purpose of *thought stopping* is self-explanatory and is used when negative thoughts and self-talk creep into your mind and try to take over. "You are so useless." "That was dumb – what did you do that for?" "I will never get this right/be able to do this/be good enough/be able to please..." "What's the point of even trying?" "I am a failure."

You can see how easily one can find themself on a negative thinking roll. Remember that negative thinking spring or spiral that perpetually rolls on and on in a downward direction? The best way to stop this seemingly out of control roll is to cut that spring. An effective way of doing this is with a short sharp "STOP!" Say it out aloud if you can, use the stop hand signal, or visualise a traffic stop sign or red traffic light. By saying "stop", a short, sharp and strong message involving the verbal domain of speech, using the physical hand movement to create a stop sign, and visually seeing or imagining a red safety stop sign or a red traffic light, you are reinforcing this message using multiple modalities, making the impact more effective.

The "stop" gives you enough of a jolt to actually interrupt your thinking momentarily and stops that negative downward spiral, cutting the spring. This provides that split second distraction from the spiral to calm yourself and realign your thinking. This combination of vocal, auditory, visual and physiological involvement is very powerful and assists in making this strategy so useful. It is a real *PEARL*; simple and easy to use, and very effective.

STRATEGY 2 Breathe

Breathing is one of my all-time favourite strategies and techniques for managing stress and anxiety; we have it with us, and therefore the capacity to use it, all of the time – and it is free! It is one of those automatic body processes that are usually managed for us by the autonomic nervous system, but we can intervene and focus on our breathing, slow it down and

take it deep into our abdomen, thus using it in a therapeutic manner. Whilst I often refer to this as the first port of call for managing stress and anxiety, from a strategy perspective, I usually adopt *Stop* as the first strategy, since stopping the negative thought spiral prior to implementing breathing makes the effect of measured or slowed breathing more beneficial.

When we are stressed or anxious we often have a feeling of winding up. Our shoulders rise or hunch, we tense our muscles and we have a general feeling of constriction. As we direct more attention to our breathing we are able to calm down by letting go of some of this stress and tension and letting the breath flow. As a result, the shoulders drop, muscles becomes more relaxed, we let go of other areas of tightness such as a clenched jaw or tense forehead, and we find we are able to re-establish a sense of balance as the stress evaporates. Stress has this feeling of pulling everything tight whilst *focused breathing* allows one to counter that by guiding you towards calmness.

Breathing more slowly and deeply enables oxygen to spread more easily throughout the entire body, whilst also ensuring that our brain is receiving all the support it needs to deal with the difficult situation at hand. Perhaps the greatest overall benefit that *breathing* offers however is its role in assisting in the process of calming our inner being, an essential ingredient for annihilating stress and anxiety.

Breathing Strategies

Some of you may be yoga experts and have mastered an array of *breathing techniques* of your own. If so, I encourage you to use those. The strategies that I'm going to outline are three of my favourite *breathing* techniques. They are intentionally simple, as they need to be easy to implement if you are going to easily implement them in times of stress.

1. **In for Three and Out for Three**
   The first technique I refer to as *in for three and out for three*. I use this as my first port of call with people who need to calm down quickly and

easily. *In for three and out for three* is pretty much what it is; breathing in for the count of one, two, three, and breathing out, two, three. This enables your breathing pattern to settle to a calmer rate. It also gives you the capability of breathing a little deeper than you were when you were stressed or under pressure. When we are stressed, we tend to breathe short and shallow gasps, breathing only through the throat and perhaps down as far as the diaphragm. The *in for three and out for three* technique enables you to breathe down to your stomach, which enables a greater intake of oxygen and assists the brain and necessary organs to prepare for managing the stress-invoking situation.

A huge benefit of *in for three and out for three* is that it doesn't require you to take breaths that are so long and focused that it is too difficult to execute. Some of the more complex strategies that require you to breathe in for five, hold it for seven, and then let it go, can be a little bit too challenging at the start but feel free to work up to more complex techniques – the more you work with your *breathing*, the calmer you will become, which is a key part of establishing that relaxed inner being that I spoke about earlier. Another advantage of *in for three and out for three* is that you can implement it anywhere; at the traffic lights, at your desk – the possibilities are endless. In a 30 second break you can take in quite a few slow breaths, which will give you the edge in developing a demeanor and inner feeling of calmness.

If you are working in customer service, it is often helpful to take a few slow *in for three and out for three* breaths between customers. It is certainly very useful if you have recently dealt with a difficult customer as it can assist you with regaining your balance before speaking to the next customer. Similarly, *breathing* can assist you with re-establishing your composure after *receiving* poor customer service. It does not take long. No one needs to (nor would they want to) know that you were taking time to re-establish your balance, but this can empower you to manage yourself so much better throughout the day.

Breathing is a PEARL – a total win-win technique.

For those choosing to work further with *breathing*, I have outlined some additional techniques that I implement for the on-going benefits of relaxation and attaining a general state of calmness.

2. **Coloured Breathing:**

   Coloured breathing is a version of *in for three and out for three* but it adds the element of colour, which creates a sensory dimension that can enhance the state of calmness. Whilst I generally use the *in for three and out for three* technique as the base, you can choose to add colour to any of your other *breathing* techniques.

   Begin by establishing your *in for three and out for three breathing.* Once your breathing pattern is established, with each breath you exhale, release the old, stale energy that has built up within. Imagine that when you breathe out for three, you are pushing out that stale energy and making room for clean, fresh energy on your next inhaling breath. Once you have that pattern established, imagine that with each breath you breathe in, you breathe in a beautiful coloured mist. The colour of the mist is your choice, but as you breathe in the mist, just visualise it spreading throughout your body, and as it does so, feel the calmness that radiates throughout your whole being. See the mist reaching all corners of your body, adding a soothing, calming, protective shield. Visualise and feel how calming that coloured mist is and how stable and smooth it makes you feel.

3. **Square Breathing**

   This strategy takes more focus and is therefore more likely to be helpful once an immediate crisis has passed. It is extremely useful when you are trying to divert your mind from ruminating, or when you are trying to sleep.

   Imagine a square with each corner being identified by a letter; A, B, C and D.

Square Breathing

4 × 4 × 4

A – Count for 4	Breathe in for 4
B – Count for 4	Breathe out for 4
C – Count for 4	Breathe in for 4
D – Count for 4	Breathe out for 4

Repeat this 4 times –
move around the square 4 times.

Repeat this exercise as often as you can; four times daily is ideal – when you awake, before bed and twice during the day.

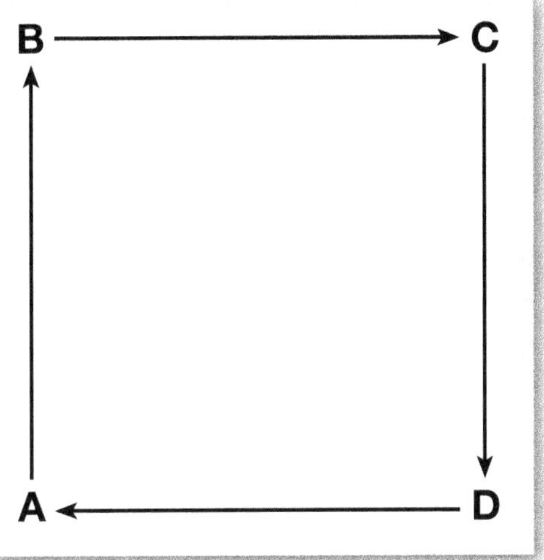

A is your starting point and as you move from A to B you breathe in for four. You breathe out for four as you move from B to C, breathe in for four between C and D and out for four between D and A.

As you move between these points, visualise moving around the square. The use of the square and the visualising serves to give your mind something to focus on, helping to remove or replace the original stressor, whilst also allowing you to focus on slowing your breathing, which assists in reducing the symptoms of stress.

STRATEGY 3 Visualisation

This is an extremely valuable skill –it is the art of taking your mind to a place that allows, enables and encourages you to feel calm. This is usually a place of tranquillity, serenity and peace, however there is no prescription for this. I often refer to this place of serenity as your *special spot*, with the main criteria being that wherever you visualise yourself, it is a pleasant and calming experience. When I am visualising for myself and taking myself to a peaceful place, I always choose a beach or an island in the sun. However, visualising can be anything for anyone. The important element is that you find a place that makes you feel calm, safe, secure, peaceful and happy.

The key to visualisation is that it provides an opportunity for your mind to switch off. This is the element that is often missing for people who become entangled in their stress, despite their best efforts at taking time out for relaxation. Many people find it relatively easy to relax physically but stopping their mind from racing can be far more difficult. Learning how to switch off or divert the mind has significant implications in many stress and anxiety-related behaviours, whilst also assisting with the quality of sleep.

STRATEGY 4 Smiles and Laughter

A long held adage has been that 'laughter is a wonderful tonic – or the best medicine'. The fact is that laughter can provide both physical and mental benefits, thereby contributing to our overall wellbeing.

As with exercise, laughter promotes our oxygen intake, stimulating our vital organs whilst releasing endorphins that contribute to our feelings of happiness[18]. Laughter also stimulates the stress response system, giving our internal organs (particularly our heart and lungs) a workout, ensuring the blood is pumping well, resulting in a feeling of enhanced relaxation. This laughter-induced muscle workout can also relieve pain from muscle spasms, which often occur during times of tension and stress, assisting physical comfort.

Whilst negative thoughts can impact the functioning of the immune system, laughter assists in reversing this trend, releasing neuropeptides that assist in combating stress, leading to positivity and wellbeing. Laughter makes us feel happier and more relaxed, thereby having a positive influence on mood.

"How can I just 'turn on' laughter, particularly when I am feeling stressed out of my mind?" you ask.

If a good belly laugh is beyond you at your point of greatest stress, start gently by aiming for something that makes you smile. For most of us there is something close to our heart that makes us smile. This might be our partner or children and for many, it is our pets. Pets have a delightful 'warm and fuzzy' innocence about them, and many people have photos of their loved ones and pets on their phone. If you do not have your partner, child, pet, favourite landscape, flower or sporting photo on your phone, consider putting one on. It takes only a few seconds to access a photo on your phone but it brings a smile, and perhaps more importantly, promotes *smile inside* feelings, which are an important contributor to positivity, and helps to reduce negativity, anxiety and stress.

STRATEGY 5 Hydration

We are increasingly aware of the benefits of hydration, particularly drinking water, and society in general drinks far more water than several decades ago, which is a healthy step forward. However, we need to be mindful of what we are drinking and how much of what types of fluid we are consuming. Whilst we are spoilt for choice when it comes to drink options, many of these are not as healthy or as helpful as we would like to think. Fruit juices are often not as natural as we expect, some being laden with sugars and preservatives, whilst coffee and tea contain stimulants, and drinking excessive amounts is linked to various negative health impacts. The fizzy drink option, whilst palatable, is not healthy as it is loaded with sugar, and even sports drinks are viewed with scepticism by some.

Regardless of our drinking preferences, we are well aware that we need to keep hydrated, and health and fitness experts constantly suggest we drink copious quantities of water.

From a stress relief perspective, maintaining our hydration is important as it provides all of our organs with the fluid they need for optimum functioning. When our bodies' function more efficiently we are better able to deal with the stresses of life, and the negative impact of stress is reduced.

Drinking water when stressed has several benefits. Physiologically it assists the functioning of our organs, and psychologically it provides an opportunity for a break or distraction from both the situation and our thoughts, which can assist to diffuse the stress.

STRATEGY 6 Go for a Walk – Remove Yourself

Removing yourself from the stressful situation is helpful (although not always possible). If you can go for a walk, the fresh air is usually helpful, providing more oxygen to the brain and other organs. Removing yourself from the situation also provides an ideal opportunity to combine the previous strategies; *Stop, Breathe, Visualise* and *Hydrate.*

Walking in itself is an extremely useful stress-reduction strategy, as exercise releases endorphins in the brain to assist in re-establishing mind-body balance. I will cover exercise in more detail later.

STRATEGY 7 Stretch

For this *PEARL* I owe a debt of gratitude to the humble domestic cat. I first became aware of the benefits of stretching many years ago after noticing the apparent delight my cat seemed to express every time he had that wonderful morning stretch. Picture the two front legs extended, pushing back on to the hind legs and then pulling himself forward through the body extending the hind legs back, right to the tip of his toes. At the completion of this fluid movement there seemed to be a feeling of complete satisfaction. Currently included in many forms of exercise, such as

yoga and pilates, there is wide recognition of the benefits of stretching, and we humans frequently attempt to imitate the ‘happy cat’ stretch.

We are also aware of the importance of stretching before and after exercise, to ensure our muscles are warm prior to the exercise, and that they cool down post-exertion. Like the cat, we humans are now also aware of how good it feels to stretch out the body. As an extension of this, we are encouraged to engage in mobility exercises during the day, particularly those in desk-bound jobs, to prevent muscle strain and spasm from either poor posture or repetitive strain injuries (RSI). This keeps our body in better condition, reduces our exposure to pain, and generally makes us feel better.

Similarly when we are feeling mentally stressed, our muscles also become tense. Stretching is a gentle and effective way of releasing muscle tension, assisting with the generalised feeling of becoming more relaxed. Stretching, as with exercise, also allows for the release of endorphins which improves mood and hence, reduces stress, whilst enhancing mind-body balance and enabling our psychological state to repair more easily. There are also physical benefits to stretching including improved circulation, increased flexibility and movement range, and reduced lower back pain.

As a strategy for the immediate relief of stress or tension, stretching is easily accessible and non-intrusive. This is another great *PEARL* to add to your stress relief strategy kit.

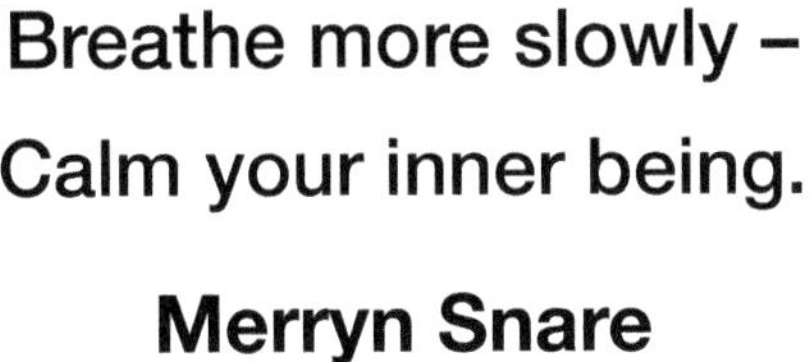

“Action is eloquence.”

William Shakespeare

CHAPTER 6

21 Stress Strategies PART 2

Lifestyle Habits

This chapter focuses on strategies that reduce both the impact of stress and your vulnerability to its escalation, and should therefore become integrated into your lifestyle. By including these *PEARLS* in your daily and weekly routine, you will be equipping your mind and body with the balance required to assist in moderating mood and enhancing positivity, which plays a pivotal role in how one deals with stress, whilst protecting you from its unnecessary accumulation.

STRATEGY 8 Regular Exercise

Exercise is a crucial element in maintaining mind-body balance. Physical and mental health are inextricably linked and we need to look after one in order to manage the other. Exercise assists in maintaining optimum health in several ways. Firstly, it assists the muscles to relax, releasing built up tension. It also stimulates blood flow to the brain, providing the nutrients essential for maintaining optimal functioning. Whilst enhancing optimal blood flow and improving the brain's efficiency, this process also assists the brain to rid its neurones of the toxic build up that occurs after sustained concentration[19,20]. For example, when someone is focused on completing a time consuming task or solving a significant problem, they are likely to expend considerable time and energy–brainpower – as they work towards completion or a solution. As a result of such sustained concentration, they are likely to experience a sense of fogginess or cloudiness in the head, feeling the need to take a break or get some fresh air. This is the result of chemical or toxic build up in the neurones and this toxicity needs to be expelled[21]. This is where exercise can assist. Typically, a person who has experienced this type of fogginess will report that they have 'cleared their head' after returning from a walk or a break in the fresh air.

Experiencing stress and/or anxiety has a similar impact to sustained concentration in that it is an intense experience, and regardless of how we might try to prevent it, whether we like it not, much of our energy is directed to our thoughts and feelings regarding the source of our concern. That's why we need to give our cognitive processing a break and

re-establish the mind-body balance. In addition to stimulating circulation and blood flow, exercise facilitates the release of endorphins, which assists in reducing negative thoughts whilst enhancing positivity[22].

Research also suggests that physically fit people cope better with stress over a longer period of time; in effect they are more resilient and able to deal with the ups and downs that stress causes[23]. This is due to the fact that their mind-body balance maintains a better synchronicity between positivity and negativity. They are also more easily able to return to a calm state if and when they are confronted by stress, keeping their daily *stress hill* in check, ensuring it does not become a *stress volcano*.

In finding the best exercise for you, aim to make it something that is relatively enjoyable and that suits your personal timetable and lifestyle. If it is too arduous, difficult to fit into your schedule, or plain boring, you simply won't stick to it. Your chosen exercise does not need to be elaborate or require expensive equipment unless that is your interest. I often suggest walking as a good place to start with exercise – it is easily accessible, cheap (you only need a decent pair of walking shoes), and you can use your lunch break if walking before or after work does not fit in with your commitments. This also ensures that people actually take their lunch break, which, as previously mentioned, is a bonus for employers and employees alike.

Swimming is another great form of exercise. It has several advantages given that the non-weight bearing nature of water exercise eliminates jarring and is gentle on the body. Swimming enables one to exercise different body parts by using different strokes, whilst swimming laps is good for cardiovascular health. There are also aqua aerobics classes, which provide sound non-weight bearing exercises and can be a useful form of physical rehabilitation post surgery or injury.

Once again, I reiterate the importance of checking with your doctor before embarking on any exercise program. Mostly, you will find your doctor

applauds you for including exercise in your routine, but it is important that the exercise regime that you choose is suitable for your medical needs and fitness level.

STRATEGY 9 Relaxation

Relaxation is an essential ingredient in managing stress, anxiety and the impact of negative thinking. It is the crucial element in ensuring that our *stress hill* is well-managed, as it provides the opportunity to seek relief from the frenetic pace of everyday demands. In short, relaxation provides the space to do whatever we need to do in order to ensure our mental fitness. To this end, relaxation is not prescriptive and can include many and varied possibilities. It may be reading a book, sitting somewhere tranquil and enjoying the scenery, having a massage, going for a run, walk or jog (although these are more likely to fit under the heading of exercise), sitting with a cup of tea, or watching your favourite show on television. The possibilities are endless and what one person finds relaxing may in fact be boring or even stressful to others.

Relaxation is perhaps more about making the time to do whatever it is that helps you to unwind and experience calmness, and the key is to make sure you do whatever you enjoy or need to do to ensure that your *stress hill* does not become the *stress volcano*.

So please, never consider relaxation an optional extra or as something to do *if* you have time. Make sure you find some time to relax regularly. See it as your well-deserved treat, and take it daily.

STRATEGY 10 Meditation

Meditation can take various forms; it can occupy significant amounts of time and, as with most things, the more you put into it, the more you are likely to benefit. However, the basic premise of meditation is to become more aware of oneself via thoughts, feelings and stillness. Rather than managing busy minds, meditation is a discipline and process for directing attention inwards and focusing on one thing, be it a thought, feeling,

vision or image. In order to achieve this, we need to master the art of ignoring distractions, which can include unwanted or unrelated thoughts, extraneous noises, or physical sensations. This notion of focusing our attention has merit for connecting with and understanding our being. However, we tend to use focus and concentration more to assist us in achieving or completing the tasks that are pressuring us – we rarely use this focus to assist in managing our stress or mental workload. To turn our attention inwards and focus on one thing of our choice provides us with the upper hand in managing how, when and where we direct our attention and energy. It also provides us with a useful tool that we can activate whenever we choose, and when we implement this several times throughout the day, we have a massive advantage in managing stress. The more time we spend purposefully directing our energy and attention, the less time we will have available for focusing on anxious thoughts that represent the misfiring of the 'fight or flight' response, and hence, there will be less opportunity to feel stressed about issues that are not within our control or truly important.

Part of the skill of meditation is to minimise the attention given to distractions. However, particularly during the learning phase, it is advisable to meditate away from distractions such as phones and noisy areas where possible. Ensure that you are physically comfortable – this might be as simple as sitting back in your chair so that your back is supported. When turning your attention inwards, many will gravitate to closing their eyes. I personally find this more comfortable, although my meditation teacher pointed out that with your eyes closed it was easier to drift off or fall asleep, and therefore meditating with your eyes closed can impair your mastery of the art of meditation. I mention that as food for thought, but give yourself the latitude to determine what will work best for you.

There is a volume of information detailing how to learn and implement meditation, and the results will, of course, vary from one person to another. Although results will be commensurate with the time and energy invested in learning and implementing this approach, it does not mean it

is essential to spend hours meditating each day. Decide what is best for you. Regardless of whether you meditate for two five minute sessions per day, whether you add some brief 30 second meditations between meetings, or whether you opt to meditate for two 20 to 30 minutes sessions daily, they will all be beneficial – the key is consistency.

STRATEGY 11 Sleep

Whilst it is well known that adequate, restful sleep is essential for maintaining good health and wellbeing, we are also aware that sound sleep patterns elude many. In short, poor sleep quality and sleep deprivation can lead to fatigue, difficulties with concentration, and accidents.

Insomnia is a common sleep disorder and its causes can vary, making it difficult to diagnose. The impact of poor sleep is significant, as our mental functioning and alertness are compromised with a flow-on impact on our productivity. Hence, the influence of sound sleep contributes to business efficiency, as well as our personal wellbeing. Whilst it is common for adults to experience the occasional poor night's sleep, persistent poor sleep occurring over several weeks has a far greater impact. Studies have found that issues with concentration and memory top the list of perceived impairment resulting from inadequate sleep, with difficulty performing hobbies, driving, using public transport, and functioning at work also featuring[24]. This highlights how intrinsically sleep is linked with our ability to do most things, but perhaps the most important link is to our safety, both in the workplace and in general living.

Sleep deprivation may result from factors including poor personal decisions (going to bed late without realising, or not considering the importance of adequate sleep), having young babies or children who are unsettled, illness, and work issues including shift work and/or work overload. Psychological issues, including stress, anxiety and depression, are also prevalent causes of insomnia, which tend to create a vicious circle for sufferers.

One of the most common concerns I hear about sleep deprivation is that people's over-active mind either prevents them from falling asleep or wakes them in the early hours of the morning, sometimes at hourly intervals. This sleep pattern becomes incredibly frustrating, as the sufferer is well aware that this is depriving them of essential sleep and so they try even harder to fall asleep, usually without success. Of course, by morning they are feeling totally drained. They drag themselves out of bed in the morning, knowing they have a full day ahead to somehow work through and then it all starts again. Sound familiar?

The key here is to learn how to manage your mind or, more specifically, your thinking. By learning how to divert your mind from the regular hurly burly of life to a place of peace and tranquillity, you are more likely to achieve peaceful and tranquil sleep. I use a relaxation based hypnosis strategy for this, which encourages and enables the 'letting go' of the mind's frenetic activity and directs it to a place of calmness. You can find more details about my hypnosis strategy and CDs in the resource section at the back of the book.

STRATEGY 12 Diet

The importance of a balanced and nutritious diet is well documented, and it is widely known that a balanced diet can assist in preventing non-communicable diseases such as diabetes, cardiovascular issues, and cancer. Whilst most people are well informed about the benefits of a balanced diet, we should be mindful of the impact modern science has made on food. The development of science and technology has seen many beneficial changes throughout the modern world, however for food production it is often a different story. In modern times there are many more additives in food and we tend to eat let less fresh produce, depriving our system of essential nutrients.

It has been found that people who regularly eat fresh fruit have a lower incidence of mental health issues, and similar results have been found

for fresh vegetables[25]. It has also been found that a balanced diet can assist in the prevention of and recovery from depression, Alzheimer's disease, attention deficit hyperactive disorder (ADHD), and schizophrenia[26]. Protein and essential fats are also important as they provide the amino acids needed for maintaining the immune system, as well as ensuring a balanced mood, which is pivotal in sound mental health[27].

In essence, the benefits of a healthy, well-balanced and fresh diet ensure that our body receives the nutrients it needs to function in the best manner possible, both physically and mentally. Maintaining alertness, clear and sound thinking, and engaging the appropriate responses to situations in the most beneficial manner, assists in managing our stress responses and provides the clarity and focus to deal with difficult situations or anxious thoughts more effectively. A balanced and regular diet assists in maintaining a level of calmness and consistency, and to this end, we need to exercise caution with regard to our intake of fats and sugars. Excessive sugar creates an initial energy boost as it is quickly absorbed into the blood stream, but such energy is usually short lived, leaving one feeling drained and fatigued. There is little to celebrate with sugar overload, which can lead to other issues such as excessive insulin production and weight gain. Similarly, we are best to avoid processed foods that are often high in additives and low in nutritional value. There is an increasing awareness about the importance of reducing or limiting our intake of processed foods, fats and sugars, but for some it is difficult to resist the easy option in deference to convenience.

Our daily diet should include fresh fruit and vegetables, protein, carbohydrates cereals and grains, dairy, and essential fats, which also need to be consumed in the correct quantities[27]. Emphasis should focus on the best quality foods available or affordable, together with the correct balance of nutrients, but if you are unsure about your diet you should consult your doctor who may refer you to a dietician.

Now that we have the *PEARLS* for great lifestyle habits, we now need the discipline to act on our knowledge.

Get it done. Tick it off.

Merryn Snare

> The greatest discovery of my generation is that a human being can alter his life by altering his attitudes of mind.
>
> **William James**

CHAPTER 7

21 Stress Strategies PART 3

Thinking About It

As discussed previously, one of the most important elements in maintaining sound mental health is to understand and, where necessary, alter our thinking. This is crucial for getting to the core of our stress and anxiety. Our beliefs and thought patterns have been forming for our entire life, and whilst changing habits can be painstaking and slow, we know that this is our decision to make – it is up to us and no one else. The *PEARLS* outlined in this section relate to thought processes, and provide some tips to assist in modifying your thought response sets if and when you choose to do so.

STRATEGY 13 Talk/Share

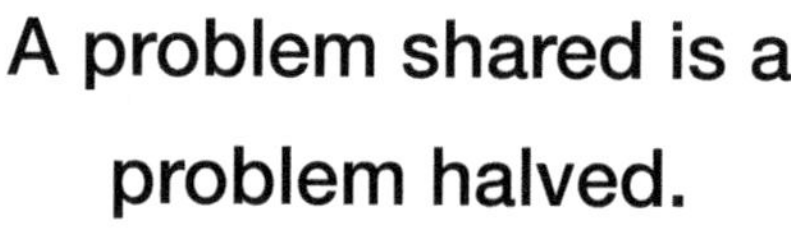

Old English Proverb

Sole ownership of a problem is onerous. Many of us think that when we have a problem it is so huge that no one else could possibly understand it, would never have felt the way we are feeling, or would even want to hear about it, let alone assist. They would probably think it so trivial we should have been able to deal with it and moved on by now. Does this sound familiar? The real key here is that these thoughts are negative, which serve to undermine self-esteem and reinforce self-criticism, spiralling down to a place of negative emotion that can lead us to unnecessary grief.

There are several options regarding with whom we might share our problems, but perhaps the most important point initially is to just share – with whomever you can or feel comfortable sharing with. Mental health professionals are well placed to assist with any mental health

issue and are often accessed with rebates from Medicare (in Australia) after an initial visit to the doctor. I am a strong believer in discussing such issues, even briefly, with your doctor as it is important for your treating doctor to have an accurate and up-to-date picture on where your world is at. In addition to your doctor, mental health practitioners who are specifically trained and have clinical expertise, are an important inclusion in your mental health picture, as they can listen to your concerns, make a relevant diagnosis where necessary, and assist you with strategies to deal with the situation. You can discuss your concerns in a private, confidential, non-judgemental and supportive environment.

Professionals can also assist in identifying maladaptive behaviours or thought patterns, such as 'catastrophising', 'black-and-white thinking', negative thought processes, and the like, whilst assisting you to develop more helpful thought and behaviour patterns. They can also assist you by reframing situations to enable you to view them differently, formulating a clear and fresh approach for a solution.

STRATEGY 14 Self-Talk

This is where your beliefs and thought processes meet the internal chatter of your mind. Self-talk might be thought of as a blend of what we have internalised from years of hearing the conversation styles that have surrounded us since we were infants. Far too often however, the theme of what we have learned is based on negativity and doubt. Key elements such as worthiness, cleverness and being 'good enough', combined with fear-related concepts surrounding failure, ensure that our self-talk is negatively biased. Remember, the clue to anxious thinking and self-talk is when you notice yourself asking "what if...?"

This "what if...?" cycle must be changed.

When working at replacing anxious or negative self-talk, consider alternatives such as; "I can...", "I have...", and so on. In doing so, it is important that expectations are set at an appropriate level – not so high that you feel

they are unattainable ("So why even bother trying"), nor so low that there is no motivation or challenge ("This is so simple I can do it without even trying"). Ensure that your expectations require a step-up from yourself, but that that step is of a reasonable increment, and back yourself to give it your best shot. Be positive and encouraging of your belief in yourself, and acknowledge and accept that you need to test your skills before you can determine your capabilities. The next important aspect is how you view mistakes – do you think of them as failures? Remember, mistakes are crucial for learning and *failing forward*; taking positive learning messages from each element that did not work as you had wished or imagined, which enables you to refine your process or strategy, enhancing your skills.

Perhaps the most forgotten element of self-talk, and one of the most important, is acknowledging you; patting yourself on the back for your positive attempts, actions and outcomes. I frequently ask my clients whether they have done this when they have been working through their personal strategies, because all too often we forget to acknowledge ourselves, our efforts, and our successes, regardless of how big or small they are.

STRATEGY 15 Positive Psychology

Positive Psychology, Gratitude and the Law of Attraction

The world of *positive psychology* owes its beginning largely to Martin Seligman, an American psychologist and educationalist who, in 1990, published his book *Learned Optimism*[28]. Optimism and pessimism are central elements to one's thinking style and play an important role in recovering from stress and anxiety. It is the ability to be attuned to when your thinking is optimistic or pessimistic that is the key and, as Seligman points out, optimism can be learned. So, we should hold much encouragement and joy in the future of optimism. Everyone, including those who are not naturally optimistic, can learn how to improve their thinking, and, as found by Seligman, the huge benefit of this is that positivity and optimism have been linked to better health and lower levels of depression[28].

Positive psychology is based on your thoughts and where the energy from your thoughts flows. It is clear that positive thinking is a much better option than that negative spring that goes on and on and usually brings us down.

It is important to celebrate our magnificent strengths, acknowledge ourselves for what we are able to do well, and to view ourselves optimistically because of what we *can* do, rather than focus on the negativity of what we believe we lack. One of the interesting distinguishing factors between optimistic and pessimistic people is that the optimists look at situations that have not resulted in the desired outcome (or 'failed') as not being something that they themselves, are solely to blame for. Optimists will look at a 'failed' situation as being a litany of events coming from an array of external sources. There may well be internal sources involved from which they can learn, but they do not see the entire failure as being attributed to them only. They have what is referred to as an *external locus of control*, believing that external factors have contributed to the outcome, whereas a pessimist believes that whenever anything goes wrong, they are solely to blame[15]. It becomes clear how this thought process feeds that negative spring which keeps spiralling downward at a rapid rate.

In a similar vein, there is currently a considerable focus in general and popular literature on the notion of gratitude – being grateful for what we have, what we can do, and what we possess. In many ways this is a simple notion and one that many of us were frequently reminded of as children, but in our younger years these reminders commonly fall on 'deaf ears' because, as children, it is difficult to understand the seemingly abstract concept of gratitude for its true meaning and value. However, the impact of gratitude is many-fold, and from a psychological and thought-processing perspective, gratitude gently highlights the benefits or privileges we are fortunate enough to have, thus directing our energy flow into positivity. The more one thinks positively, the less energy one has to direct towards the negativity that impedes our personal development

and progress. This is where *positive psychology* and *gratitude* link with the *Law of Attraction*, since a large part of the assertion from the *Law of Attraction* suggests that where you concentrate your thoughts is also where you are concentrating your energy, and it is this concentration of energy that leads to outcomes – good or bad.

Esther and Jerry Hicks are prolific writers with many books and audio books available on the *Law of Attraction*, which deal largely with how one's energy flow and thoughts attract what they are focused towards[29]. The contention is that if you are focusing on negative things, you are likely to attract negative things. If you focus on positive things, life can become really exciting and fulfilling.

Mike Dooley is another author who believes in the *Law of Attraction* and that one can think their way to good things[30,31,32]. He has a wonderful saying; "Thoughts become things … choose the good ones!" This can be a useful way to think about how you direct your energy and your thoughts and, as such, help develop positive thinking styles and positive self-talk. Simply taking time to reflect on what we have to be grateful for is a useful way of managing our thinking and putting stressful events into perspective.

American-Israeli educator, Tal Ben-Shahar, is another proponent of *positive psychology*. A simple activity that Tal spoke about in a lecture that I attended, which is probably something many of us already do without realizing it, is to think of the good things that have occurred during the day, every day[33,34]. Tal uses this approach with his children, asking them about their favourite things from the day before they go to bed at night, which is a wonderful strategy to teach children, but is also a strategy equally beneficial for people of any age.

This is a strategy that I have used for a very long time and Tal's lecture reminded me of just how powerful this strategy is. An example of how I have used this is with my daughter, when she was becoming increasingly

annoyed and critical of one of her teachers. This was the first time I had been aware of her not liking a teacher so I said to her, "You can tell me everything you want to about this teacher, and everything you don't like about her, but before you do, I want you to tell me *three good things* about her." So she proceeded, somewhat sarcastically at first, but this process enabled her to move to a place where, in a short period of time, she actually came to understand this teacher. Whilst venting can be an important part of letting go of stress, if we can also learn to be aware of the *two pairs of shoes* as we vent, once we have settled a little, we can aim to find something positive about the person who might be irritating us or contributing to our stress. We are then able to gain a more accurate and helpful assessment of the situation, improving our perspective and reducing our stress. In this scenario, my daughter was able to grasp the *two pairs of shoes* principle, and began to understand this teacher and her situation, and actually came to like and respect her.

I use this *three good things* strategy with many of my clients, and when they implement this strategy regularly, they find it is very effective in assisting them to change their thinking from pessimistic to optimistic. Some clients are extremely diligent and try to think of three different things every day, and if you are able to do that it will broaden your positive outlook significantly, as your mind becomes increasingly aware of the many wonderful things that surround you. However, I don't necessarily think there needs to be three different things each day. A gratitude that occurs every day for me is my morning shower – the joy of hot water. I am eternally grateful for the fact that we have the ability to have a warm or hot shower and I find that the ease with which we can access hot water is fantastic.

Now that you can see how simple gratitude can be, you will be able to think of many things in your own world for which you are grateful. Initially I think it is best to write what you are giving gratitude for in a notebook or gratitude diary. Writing has the effect of cementing the

habit and sharpens your focus on the positivity of the strategy, enabling you to truly embrace optimistic thinking.

Whilst many of you may use this strategy, using it with greater focus and intention is an effective but simple way of ensuring your thinking style becomes more positive and optimistic, equipping you to more easily annihilate stress and anxiety.

STRATEGY 16 Acceptance

There are two increasingly popular psychological treatments that are built around the notion of acceptance – firstly *Mindfulness* and secondly *Acceptance and Commitment Therapy (ACT)*[11]. In essence, these approaches are about the recognition and awareness of how one might be feeling in response to given events, whilst allowing the event's impact to pass. Acceptance implies one is able to either agree with the outcome of an event, or to recognise that the outcome will not be altered whether they agree with it or not. To this end, there is an overlap in meaning with tolerance, although to consider that acceptance is the same as tolerance is not accurate. With regard to stress, acceptance of a situation can be the most effective way of reducing one's stress and associated discomfort. Whilst you may not agree with a behaviour, event or outcome, to accept it, let it go, learn something from it, and move on, can be the best way forward for you and possibly for others as well. In essence, acceptance fits with the *different ≠ wrong* notion, and whilst there may be times when you strongly believe another *is* wrong, deferring to the acceptance of different points of view and the *two pairs of shoes* theory has a positive outcome for your stress levels.

Change is very do-able.
It merely requires that
you take action.

Merryn Snare

"Stress is an ignorant state.
It believes that everything
is an emergency.
Nothing is that important."

Natalie Goldberg

CHAPTER 8

21 Stress Strategies PART 4

The *Essential Elements*

This is the final group of stress-annihilating strategies, with the two concluding strategies encompassing what I consider to be the essential overview to empowering yourself to annihilate stress and anxiety. Whilst the 'thinking' group may be considered the most pivotal in annihilating stress and anxiety in the long-term, the *essential elements and the PEARLS of resilience* (strategies 20 and 21) are important keys to maintaining the lifestyle routine that will ensure you remain in charge of your thoughts and responses.

Before I detail these key overviews, I will outline some additional strategies that can be helpful in assisting the management of your stress.

Personal Preferences

STRATEGY 17 Friends – Social Interactions

When we are feeling stressed or anxious, one of the common behaviours that typify this state is withdrawal from friends or social interaction. So why do we do it? Perhaps it is because we are grappling with what is happening – we may not be feeling quite right and we are unable to put it into words. If we can't articulate what we are feeling for ourselves, how could we possibly discuss it with anyone else? Herein lies an important clue. If and when you notice that your social interactions are declining, especially if you are declining invitations or you are not enjoying doing the things you once did, this might be indicative that you are struggling with stress, anxiety or depression. The hint is the change in behaviour, and the sooner you notice this pattern and act on rectifying it, the better and more comfortable, more 'normal' or more like your 'old self' you will feel.

The fact is that if we were to share our problem(s) with a trusted friend or relative, they would absolutely want to assist in any way they could (given that they are a trusted friend or relative!), so what is it that holds us back? Our thinking! This becomes our self-talk, that is probably telling us all manner of negative things, and when we are feeling burdened we

tend to become more negative and we don't see the obvious. *Of course, our friends and family want to help us and be there for us.*

Strategy 18: Music

Music, particularly classical music, has long been considered a helpful way to unwind, relax, de-stress or to express one's inner being. The creativity in the writing and development of musical scores has afforded us an amazing range of choice spanning a continuum from gentle, relaxing, meditative styles, to light, catchy rhythms and rhyme, jazz and blues, and rock or heavy metal styles. Individual preferences are likely to vary, depending on your situation, time and space.

Whilst there are limited clinical studies dedicated to considering the link between music and stress relief, results of those that have been conducted suggest that music has a positive recovery impact on the autonomic nervous system and a positive influence on recovery from the psychological stress response[35]. Music has also been found to reduce the awareness or sensation of pain and discomfort in children and adults, as well as assist in improving mood and some symptoms of depression, and it can also improve the co-ordination and communication of children[36].

It is interesting to note that music is often used to accompany meditation. These musical scores are often purpose-written, but encompass gentle rhythms and melodies, which are frequently infused with the sounds of nature e.g. running water, the distant chirping of birds, and gentle animal sounds. Classical music is also frequently used for relaxation, with the calming and soothing qualities assisting people in allowing their thoughts to flow with the music, facilitating the release of stress. Having said that, some people take themselves to a place of freedom by listening to their favourite pop, rock, or jazz music, or whatever makes them feel 'pumped.' Whilst the relaxation of classical music works for some, others benefit from lifting their demeanour, almost as if the rhythm and

melody of their favourite music lifts them from a place of flatness to a place of energetic endeavour. There are no rights and wrongs; it is personal preference and if music helps you to de-stress, then go for it!

Whatever our preferences, mood or situation, music has the potential to move us to a different space – the rhythm and rhyme seems to provide both the structure and freedom that we need at a given point in time and also encourages a release of tension through self-expression. As a stress relief strategy, music is more easily accessed than ever. Most people can access their favourite music on their phone or MP3 player without disrupting others, so it can be easily and readily accessed, and may also be considered as an immediate relief strategy.

STRATEGY 19 Television

Watching a favourite television show can be one's regular relaxation or 'unwind' for the day. For some it is about vegging out in front of the television. Others are inspired by documentaries and thrive on learning about new facts and figures that are non-work related and afford a complete change of thought or pace of the working day. Others like to watch drama or sci-fi thrillers as yet another form of escapism, whilst comedy and a good belly laugh is the change of pace preferred by others. We are spoilt for choice in many ways, with a range of free-to-air digital channels, as well as pay television, DVDs, and online movie choices. For others however, television is nothing but a load of noise and in order to unwind, their preference may be to leave the television off. It is all a matter of personal choice – and the choice is yours.

The Essential Elements

STRATEGY 20 Feed Your Energy

Establishing and maintaining a balanced life is essential for optimum mental and physical health and a sound quality of life. Prevention of burnout is a key benefit of maintaining this balance, as is the ability to ensure the on-going efficiency and productivity in all aspects of one's

life. This is also reflected in the workplace, and it is the concept of balance that needs to be integrated into our complete being.

People often expect to be able to give out high levels of energy and effort to their family, friends and social networks, as well as their work, without taking any time to adequately recover or restore their energy. It doesn't work like that! When you constantly give out energy and effort, your energy reserves diminish and you need to bolster the supply. I refer to this as *feeding your energy*. Some clients protest that they feel they are being selfish if they take time for themselves. My answer? You won't be able to assist or support anyone if you have completely exhausted your energy and are flat out on your sickbed! It is not selfish to re-hydrate your energy. Furthermore, it is essential to do so if you are going to continue supporting the people around you in the manner you have been doing or would like to do.

The diagram on the following page illustrates how to ensure you *feed your energy.*

Whilst most of the elements of *feeding your energy* have been discussed previously as separate strategies, they increase their power many fold when combined in this routine and integrated into your approach to daily living. *Feed your energy* is about prevention, and if you adopt this strategy as part of your daily life, you are far less likely to be bothered by stress and anxiety. For this reason, I suggest focussing on five key areas: diet, exercise, sleep, relaxation and fun. Yes fun! Do you remember what that is? All too often we become so entrapped in satisfying the needs of others, that we almost forget what it is like to experience fun – or relaxation for that matter – for ourselves.

Let us revise these elements one by one:

Diet and nutrition is relatively straightforward. Ensure you maintain a well-balanced diet, enjoying treats such as sugars, chocolate, caffeine and alcohol in moderation. If you have particular dietary requirements

Feed Your Energy

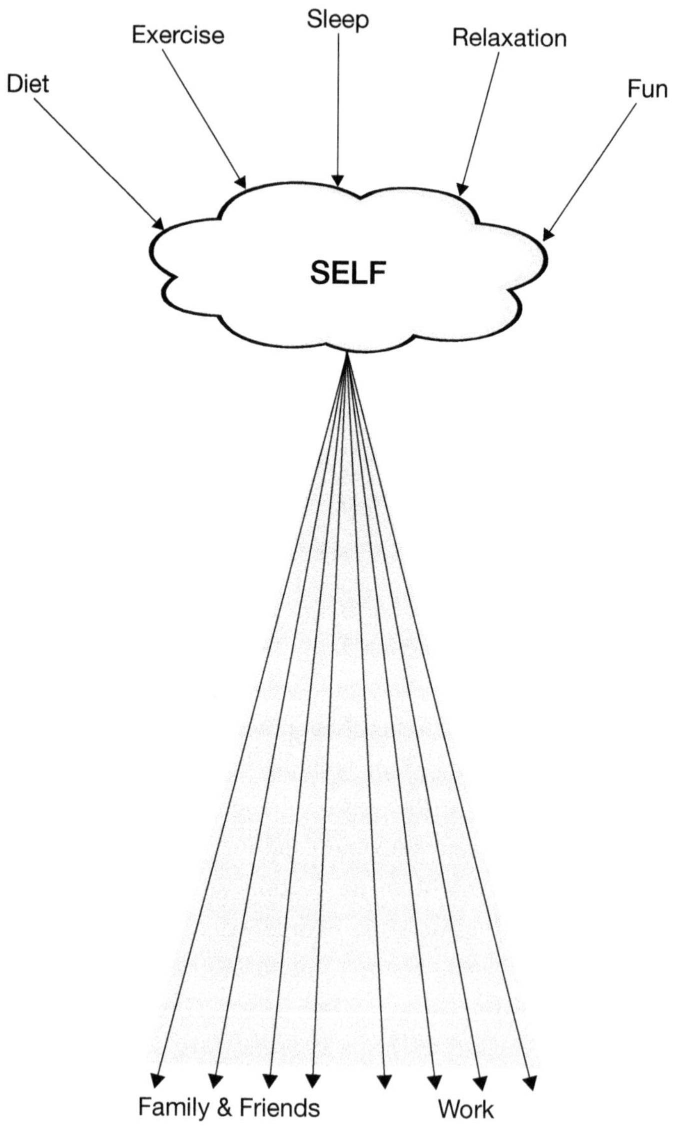

Diet

Exercise

Sleep

Relaxation

Fun

SELF

Family & Friends

Work

based on medical needs, ensure that you stick to them – consistently. Just as you must put the appropriate type of fuel into your car, diet and nutrition is about putting appropriate fuel into your body.

Exercise is also easily understood – maintain a regular exercise regime that is suitable for your physical and medical condition. Frequently, the most difficult part is actually doing it, so remember that famous tick slogan and make sure you "just do it" – regularly.

Sleep is a concern for many, and whilst the majority of people function best when they have six to eight hours sleep, individuals have a wide range of needs. The fact remains, however, that there are many people who are troubled by dysfunctional sleep patterns. Using the strategies discussed in the previous section, aim to establish a regular and uninterrupted sleep pattern that provides you with the hours of sound sleep that are optimal for your needs. I have a seven to eight hours sleep per night need – what is yours?

Relaxation, whilst often aligned with sleep, deserves its own focus. This encompasses time for you to do whatever you enjoy. Some people find social catch-ups relaxing, others prefer to read a book or have a massage. Others still find physical activity relaxing. In this context, relaxation refers to whatever gives you down time, or the opportunity to focus on whatever you want, as long as it is just for you.

Fun is not usually associated with stress and anxiety, and is therefore an important inclusion as an antidote for stress, or more precisely, as prevention to the build up of stress. Fun can provide a release from the work and/or stress elements that occupy much of one's being (where work might relate to the home as well as the workplace). In addition, fun is a great way to socialise, it elicits laughter which has physiological benefits, and facilitates positive thinking, all of which are wonderful attributes for annihilating stress.

In short, fun should be simply great fun!

STRATEGY 21 The PEARLS of Resilience

The golden key to annihilating stress and anxiety is the awareness of change in specific behaviours. If we develop a deeper awareness and understanding of ourselves – how we think, feel and act – and we are mindful of changes to any of these elements, we need to identify what changed and why; what is the reason for the change, what is different in my world, and what is making me feel different from how I used to feel?

Frequently, people who don't sleep well find their mind is over-active. Concerns tend to flood in at the time they need it least and they ruminate around and around in circles, searching for answers and depriving them of precious sleep. Does this sound familiar? From here the regular exercise routine becomes less regular, the mind quickly justifying it as a need to reset and catch up on that missed sleep. It also seems that the regular healthy diet has slipped, as you feel too tired, stressed or time-poor to even think about preparing that healthy salad or home cooked meal that you usually enjoy. You also find that you are becoming increasingly irritated and grumpy, which is annoying and frustrating, as it is not really like you. Your partner or friends may also be finding that you are not so much fun to be with, or worse still, your children may have become scared of your reactions, believing that they might have made you annoyed with them but not understand what they have done.

Does any of this ring true for you? Has it in the past?

These are the vital symptoms of change that can be indicative of a significant stress build-up. It is another version of *over-the-shoulder stress,* the stress that builds up behind you ever so gradually and you don't see it coming. Suddenly you find yourself struggling; not managing to keep up at work, lacking the energy and enthusiasm for everything at work and at home, feeling as though you are on the verge of a meltdown or collapse, and you have no idea why! There have been no significant changes or negative events, so why are you feeling the way you do?

Over-the-shoulder stress has struck and the truth is, it has probably been building for some time – you just didn't notice.

To protect yourself from this, you need to understand and implement *the PEARLS of resilience,* monitoring and managing any changes before they run rampant. *The PEARLS of resilience* are intended as a lifestyle framework and keeping each element in check will enable you to maintain personal balance and wellbeing. The *PEARLS* are detailed below and represent your personal key and essential overview of your mental health.

P – Personal balance

E – Eating habits

A – Activity

R – Relaxation

L – Logical thought processes

S – Sleep

Monitor these *PEARLS* regularly, and by ensuring that they do not move too far beyond their usual boundary, you will have a great chance at protecting yourself from the silent escalation of *over-the-shoulder stress.*

> **Over-the-shoulder stress creeps up without you noticing.**
>
> **Merryn Snare**

Human beings, by changing the inner attitudes of their minds, can change the outer aspects of their lives.

William James

CHAPTER 9

Effective Strategy Combinations

Whilst each of these 21 strategies or *PEARLS* is useful and effective on its own, they often reinforce each other and as a result, have more power when used in combination. I will share some stories to illustrate this and to provide insight into how my clients and I have adapted and combined these strategies to create a solid platform to annihilate their stress and anxiety.

People's Stories: 1

Andy is a young, 22-year-old man who came to see me because he was feeling overwhelmed with where his life was heading. He described himself as usually being a positive or 'up' person, but was finding that in recent times he was taking a negative view of things all the time, and he was uncomfortable with this.

Andy is a delightful young man who likes to do the right thing, tries hard, and, like most of us, is learning as he goes.

He was working as a trainee in a new job and he started to become anxious at work because he was learning a range of new tasks, some of which were difficult to master. We talked about his situation, about what was reasonable, and what was part of the learning process, but we also used a number of strategies to help Andy manage his feelings of overwhelming stress.

In effect, Andy's stress had built up to the point where he was undermining his own ability to work in the way that he knew he could. He was allowing things to get on top of him and he found himself winding himself down into that negative downward spiral.

Some of the strategies we put in place for Andy were, first of all, to teach him how to use *breathing* to try and keep him in a calm space. I wanted him to learn that if he could slow down his breathing, it would slow down how everything else functioned. It would slow down his racing mind, allow his body recover, and it would enable him to think

things through in a calmer manner than he had been doing, which would ultimately enable him to make better decisions.

Andy's first task whenever he felt upset, was to take a few moments out, and to count his breaths, breathing in, two, three, and out, two, three. This is the *breathing in for three and out for three* strategy, and in Andy's case was implemented before the *'stop'* strategy as becoming calm was initially a higher priority than dissecting his thought patterns. I wanted Andy to learn to function in a calm space which I thought was the single most important change that would enhance both his workplace performance and his confidence.

(*PEARL* #2)

Andy took this homework seriously and he told me that he did his *breathing* at his tea breaks to try and help himself stay in a calmer space throughout the day. This is a really important point, as working at maintaining an overall state of calmness assists in preventing yourself from getting too worked up when the going gets tough. Maintaining relative calmness provides a sound basis so that when upsetting things occur, whilst it is normal to react, there will be sufficient room in your *stress hill* to deal with or cope with the stressors before your coping resources are stretched to the point of the erupting volcano.

Andy still found that he was stressed sometimes, and he used his *breathing* to help calm down, but the next thing we needed to do was to work on his thinking to stop the negative thoughts, which as so frequently occurs, was taking Andy into a downward spiral. From here we added the thought-stopping technique "*stop*" to *breathing,* which creates the strategy I refer to as *stop and breathe.*

This is a combined strategy of *stop* and *breathing,* which requires the individual as soon as they becomes aware of a negative thought, to cut it, thereby preventing the negative spiral from taking hold. Once you

stop that negative train of thought, you also have the cue to bring in your *breathing–in for three and out for three*. The *breathing* helps to settle your stress and anxiety. The stopping of that negative thought gives you that split second to realign your thinking and to re-direct your thinking from that negative downward track onto a more even keel and then on to a more positive track.

(*PEARLS* #1, 2)

The next thing that Andy and I worked with was his thinking. It was very important for him to understand his past thinking structures – the way he has always interpreted things or perceived things – and to look at what life events might have influenced the way he thinks.

Certainly, much of how we think comes from what is modelled to us as children by our parents, families, teachers and other significant leaders in our world. The development of our unique thinking structures is influenced by the positivity and encouragement we receive. Another part of it comes from who we are –our personality style – and very often, our thinking structures or patterns as adults reflect childhood events and experiences.

Hence, we need to decipher which of our thought patterns are serving us well and which are inhibiting or damaging our growth and development, in order to determine which parts of our thinking, or which response styles, need to change. Changing one's thinking fits into the CBT strategy of challenging our negative thoughts. To achieve this, it is important to be clear on what you are actually saying to yourself. Andy identified his negative thoughts and learned how to stop them, and then to reframe them so they soon lost their power and impact.

Another important aspect for Andy regarding his thinking was looking at the pressure he felt when he made mistakes at work. One of the complex issues around making mistakes in an external environment

is the influence of other people; where their stress levels are at, how they manage their stress, their personality style, and how they behave in general. This often comes into play, particularly in the workplace, but is also common in social friendship groups. Part of the learning is about how to deal with other people who perhaps are playing out their own stresses and making life miserable for someone else. It would seem that this is partially what's going on in Andy's working life. However, he also has things to learn and he also makes mistakes sometimes, which is what I consider a normal part of the learning curve. In short, we have to keep *failing forward* or making mistakes, with each attempt being that little bit better.

So, when anyone is learning the art of *failing forward* as they develop new skills, yes, it is acceptable, understandable and natural to make mistakes; just make sure that you learn from them. It is also important to challenge your thinking about making mistakes, because too often people *awfulize* or have *catastrophic* thinking where they put pressure on themselves to never, ever make a mistake because that is just the worst thing possible. Does this sound familiar?

(*PEARLS* #13, 14)

Andy learned much about his thinking. He learned how to challenge his thoughts and how to actually put a positive view on what he had previously been thinking of in a negative way. In essence, many of the mistakes he was making at work were a natural part of that learning curve that we all encounter when we take up a new job, task or activity.

(*PEARL* #16)

As Andy progressed through the process of understanding his thinking, stopping his negative thought spirals, and finding the ability to reinstate a feeling of calmness when he had been reverting to panic,

another strategy that I wanted to introduce was for him to diarize his days. By writing about what went well and what didn't each day, and giving himself a score for out of five each day, where five was a really great day and one was a pretty ordinary day, would provide a more tangible overview of his progress, rather than relying upon memory, which may become influenced by the emotions of a particularly good or bad day. The other huge advantage with diarizing and giving oneself a daily overview score is that you can check your progress over time.

One of the foundations for bringing Andy's stress levels down – and this is probably the case for most people – is to be able to have more relaxation time in the day and your week. Relaxation is one of the things that helps prevent that *stress volcano* from erupting. If we have daily relaxation techniques that we can bring into our life, the daily stresses and strains that we may experience can be neutralized.

(*PEARL* # 9)

After teaching Andy how to use the *stop and breathe* technique, I added another strategy – *visualization.* I wanted Andy to *stop and breathe* to enable him to find a calmer space. Before he got back into directing his thoughts onto work, I wanted him to *visualize* being in a place that he loves to be – a place that he would naturally find soothing, pleasant and calming. I wanted Andy to find his own *special spot.* For homework I asked Andy to start adding the *visualization* strategy of his *special spot* to his *stop and breathe* technique.

(*PEARLS* #1, 2, 3)

Combining the *visualization* strategy with *breathing* to assist him in staying calm when a stressful situation had arisen, together with Andy's awareness of his past thinking style which he was now able to challenge and therefore change, Andy was now moving into a space where he was

increasingly able to manage his stress. This was empowering for him, which also helped to reduce his stress even further.

A key point for anyone experiencing stress, anxiety or panic is the reassurance that comes from knowing that they have the skills and strategies to cope. This prevents the fear associated with the stress, anxiety or panic from escalating, and re-affirms the positivity gained through having the coping resources to manage what otherwise might have been a difficult situation.

The next thing that we looked at was the *positive psychology* element of *gratitude*. This is something that we all should be considering, whether we are stressed or not, and it does not need to be complex. I asked Andy to write three things that were good about the day, each day. This could be done at the beginning of the day, recounting for the previous day, or in the evening. I also wanted it written, rather than merely thought about. Andy did this homework. He learned to find gratitude in days that were sometimes pretty difficult. He did a fabulous job, keeping a diary about what was good in his day, and he found himself looking for three different things every day. He was really challenging and stretching himself.

(*PEARL* # 15)

An important point to emphasize is that these tasks may sound simple, and on one level they are. However, they can also be difficult to implement consistently, which is what is required to change you thinking and change your habits. Stick with it. If you find you are not implementing a strategy as consistently as you would like, do not give up. Keep at it.

As I wanted Andy to spend more of his thinking space on a positive or neutral level, as opposed to a negative level, I was looking to give him additional strategies that would make his *smile inside*. An effective way of doing this is to use photographs, and with the popularity of

devices such as smartphones that can record so many things, including photographs, this is a really useful tool.

I talked to Andy about what he really loved and what sorts of things made him *smile inside*. Andy showed me photos of his dog, which instantly brought out his smiles and his laughs. I wanted him to capture this during the working day, and suggested that he spend some time during his breaks to look at the photos of his dog on his phone –anytime where he could take 30 seconds to reinvigorate his smile. Andy did this, and he enjoyed it, and found that with all of these things together, he was feeling far less anxious and stressed, and felt that he had a far more realistic approach to where his life was at.

(*PEARL* #4)

The other thing that I encouraged Andy to do was talk with his manager, because part of his stress – and probably a significant part – came from feeling that he wasn't doing a good enough job, and given that he was training in his new job, he needed to make a success of it. He spoke to his boss and discovered that he was really happy with his work. As it turned out, Andy's boss wanted him to work on building his confidence, which was a large part of what we had been working with. The interesting point here is that when our thinking is not serving us well, the ramifications almost always include the undermining of our confidence, which adds fuel to that negative thinking spiral.

(*PEARL* #13)

Andy is about to move jobs to a new trainee position as his previous employer is moving and has no opportunity to provide him with ongoing employment. He now feels confident within himself, and, by his own admission, believes he has the strategies to move forward and no longer needs to see me. Great work Andy.

People's Stories: 2

Margaret, a lady in her late 70s, came to see me because she was struggling to cope with the fact that her husband, in his mid 80s, was in declining health. There had recently been a rollercoaster of ups and downs with his health, and whilst he was relatively stable at the time she first saw me, Margaret feared that at some point, she would be outliving him. Her concerns were, that apart from the prospect losing her life partner, and managing both the loss and accompanying grief, she was becoming increasingly panicky about how she would cope living alone. Margaret and her husband appeared to have a very deep love and bond with each other, and functioned as a dedicated team.

Margaret's anxiety was not unusual, and if we consider her generation and age group, where men and women often had defined roles, the prospect of being alone and having to manage everything single-handedly becomes extremely daunting. For those of Margaret's generation, there are likely to be areas such as finance, external house maintenance and the like, where the majority of women have had neither the desire nor the need to understand how they operated, unlike the people of Gen X, Gen Y and, to a lesser extent, Baby Boomers. Hence, the feeling of being overwhelmed spilled from the emotional to the practical, and easily became all encompassing.

As a result, Margaret was feeling extremely concerned and frightened for her future without her husband, which culminated in her feeling very 'dark and blue'. My first step was to listen to Margaret's story, enabling me to hear and understand what was happening on a practical, psychological and emotional level. This is crucial as people really need to both be and feel heard. Nobody wants to feel pushed into treatment options without actually feeling that their story has been understood, and without this connection, treatment is not likely to be successful. We talked about how Margaret was feeling and I also talked about how people generally find, from some inner strength, a way of managing in such difficult and changing circumstances, which gave her a glimmer

of hope. I wanted Margaret to grasp that glimmer of hope to protect her from potentially winding down in a spiral of negativity. It was important that she believed in herself, whilst acknowledging the reality of her situation and the normality of her concerns.

(*PEARL* #13)

We ascertained from the outset that Margaret's diet was nutritionally sound and consistent, and she was enrolled in sound exercise regimes. Her sleep was not great, but this had not changed significantly due to her recent stressors. When we considered the *feed your energy* diagram, the areas of relaxation and fun were the missing links, for whilst Margaret and her husband were generally quite sociable, of late there was a 'can't be bothered' feeling. Margaret was also feeling so stretched in terms of her personal resources that she felt she had no time to think of herself.

(*PEARLS* #8, 11, 12, 20)

From here we looked at identifying the stressors that were concerning her, teasing out the specifics. What were the real issues that she feared she would not be able to cope with in the future, and what were issues for her at the present time? From here we considered what Margaret might be able to change – it was important for her to recognise that she still had control over some aspects of her life, despite the overwhelming feelings associated with loss of control regarding her husband's declining health. This notion of change, especially when applied to habits of a lifetime, can be overwhelming. Often people don't like the idea of changing their routines and their patterns, especially if they feel it is a forced change. It was also hard work, but Margaret was receptive to the idea of modifying some aspects of her routine, and at the start of her treatment journey we identified what small steps and changes she could make to improve the quality of her time with her husband and her life in general.

Initially, I introduced the concept of *positive psychology* and *gratitude,* and I encouraged Margaret to tell me about the things that she had in her life that were good. Although there were areas in her life that she feared, there were still some positives and she, like most grandparents, very proudly told me about her three grandchildren. The first homework task I asked of Margaret was to focus on gratitude, and to take some time each day to focus on what was good in her life. I asked her to keep a journal, diary or notebook to record her gratitude daily, by writing about three positive things every day. Once again, the key here was simplicity. Keeping things simple is important. It gets back to the notion of taking time out to 'smell the roses' or enjoy the simple pleasures of life. In the hurly-burly world of today, and given the changes occurring in Margaret's world, it is too easy to forget about the simple pleasures.

(*PEARLS* #10, 12, 15)

Margaret, like Andy, tried to write something different every day, so during her second visit I asked her to simplify it and take it down a notch. Wow – the homework gets easier!

Another issue that arose for Margaret was what I refer to as *low vibe days*. Some days she found that she just felt flat. She couldn't pick herself up and she just felt 'not great'. This happens to most people from time to time, and I think it is unrealistic for us to expect ourselves to be 'up' all the time. We talked about *low vibe days,* and how some days might be flat, boring and uninteresting, but that it's important to accept that this is part of the normal ups and downs of life. When we talk about normal ups and downs, we are aware that this is the pattern or journey of life. It is avoiding the very deep peaks and troughs that we are aiming for. Our goal is to flatten out the deep peaks and troughs. Once Margaret understood and accepted the notion of *low vibe days*,

together with the reality that the next day was likely to be better than the *low vibe day,* and the fact that she had now normalised that process, it became easier for her to move forward.

(*PEARL* #13)

As Margaret reflected on and analysed the contributing stressors in her world, she realised that apart from the enormity of her husband's health, on a day-to-day basis she was becoming increasingly overwhelmed at having to cook meals every day. Once again, if we consider Margaret's generation, there is an expectation that women will prepare healthy meals for their husbands every night. In current times this might be more of a self-expectation rather than a societal expectation, but regardless of the origin of the expectation, it had become a chore and a bore, and it was now at the point where it was putting too much pressure on her. In conjunction with the pressure that she felt about her husband's health, this seemed to be almost tipping her over the edge.

We discussed alternatives to Margaret being the sole cook, and one of her homework tasks was to research where she could get meals that would suit their medical needs, such as diabetic requirements, and to find out what she could afford in terms of prepackaged meals. I suggested a number of alternatives including frozen meals from the supermarket, but I also wanted her to research private companies or kitchens that provide this service and also cater to specific dietary needs. Margaret diligently investigated these options and found a brand of catering that fitted with their dietary needs and that she could afford to utilise once or twice a week, which really took the pressure off her. Margaret found that just knowing that she no longer had to provide a meal every night made all the difference. In fact, with this option in place, it was something in her week that she looked forward to; "the night where our dinner is prepared for us".

(*PEARL* #18)

I asked Margaret to focus on tuning in to her thoughts and feelings when she was feeling down or flat, and to ask herself, "What am I feeling? Why am I feeling it?" I wanted her to be specific in identifying what those thoughts and feelings were. Was it because everything felt overwhelming or was there a particular focus that we could work with? Was it a *low vibe day,* which she could now identify and perhaps ignore in the knowledge that tomorrow was likely to be different, or was there a particular stressor that we needed to understand and deal with? I was aiming for Margaret to develop a greater awareness of her feelings, which, as we know, are connected to our thinking. When we are aware of our thoughts and feelings we are in a better space to work at changing what is not serving us well.

I now wanted to introduce the notion of *thought stopping*, to encourage Margaret to understand the impact of her negative thinking. I asked Margaret to focus on learning how to breathe gently, and we practiced together *breathing in for three and out for three.* I wanted to ensure that she took time out to check her breathing, to settle things down and to avoid winding up in a volcanic stress attack. We then added *visualisation* to the *breathing,* and for Margaret that was something as simple as being outside in the garden and enjoying the beautiful flowers. She and her husband both love the garden and this was a really calming and soothing place for her. Enhancing the strength of this strategy for Margaret was the fact that she could visualise being in the garden, or she could physically take herself out to the garden. She found that this actually helped her to stay calm.

(*PEARL* #1, 2, 3)

Margaret's husband experienced another stroke in between two of our sessions and as difficult and traumatic as it was, Margaret noticed that she handled it better than she would previously have expected and she put it down to the fact that she was learning from her experience;

she had been there before, she had managed before, and she would manage again. Reinforcing our past efforts and experiences reminds us that we *can* manage the difficult times, which is a crucial part of thinking for everyone.

Margaret worked diligently at recognising her negative thinking, and for much of the time was able to use the *stop and breathe* technique to change the negative into positive thoughts. Margaret recognised and reframed her thinking to reflect that although there are things that are not great and it is extremely difficult when your partner is ill, there are also some things in her life that are good. The regular use of a gratitude diary assisted Margaret in maintaining a focus on positive thinking, given that she now accepts that her husband's health is in decline and there will always be medical concerns. She is now able to moderate her stress by using *positive psychology* and *gratitude*, rational and positive thinking, and *visualisation*. Margaret now has more confidence in herself and the ability to manage whatever occurs in the future. This, I think, is an amazing achievement, and I congratulate her.

(*PEARLS* #1, 2, 3, 4, 12, 13, 14, 15, 16, 20)

People's Stories: 3

Lauren is a 25-year-old university graduate who came to see me about a needle phobia. Lauren has a medical condition that requires monitoring with periodic blood tests to ensure that her health is in the best possible space. However, she found that she was becoming increasingly anxious, teary and tending to freak out at the thought of having blood tests, which she believed was because of the needle. This was impacting on not only her health condition but her general health as well, and, as a result, she realised she needed to do something about it.

(*PEARL*#13)

Lauren is a generally fit and healthy girl, apart from her underlying stress-related condition. Her exercise regime and diet were well-balanced and regular, and she generally slept well.

(*PEARLS* #8, 11, 12)

As you are now aware, a crucial and basic strategy for everyone's stress management is *breathing*; we have it with us all the time – we just need to learn how to regulate it to serve us. It is a super-convenient strategy which can be implemented anywhere, and can be done almost without anyone knowing. Hence, it is usually one of the key starting points for most of my clients, for by establishing a *breathing technique* at the outset, they are in a calmer headspace and more easily able to work through their issues, adopting other strategies as required.

(*PEARL* #2)

I also worked with Lauren using hypnosis, which is something that you should always undertake with a trained practitioner. However, as Lauren brought some interesting thought processes and adaptations into her routine that fit the general realm of managing stress, I felt there were key learning points that would be useful considerations for your own stress management regime.

We talked about where Lauren was at with needles, some of the factors that might have been influencing why she felt the way she did, and why she became so upset about them. We used hypnosis for Lauren to move back in time to find out how she reacted to needles as a child. As Lauren was talking through her story and situation, I encouraged her to check her *breathing* and slow it down so that she could stay calmer as she was thinking things through. What Lauren discovered was that she, herself, did not particularly have an issue with the needles. It was more the reactions and demeanor of people around her that caused her stress;

family members when she was young, and in a more recent experience it seemed that it was the demeanor of the nurse that upset her, leading her thinking into a negative spiral that took her to a place of extreme discomfort. In fact, Lauren now believed it was not really the needle as such that triggered her stress and anxiety, but more a collection of elements that all contributed to the blood test process. From here, Lauren realised that letting go of the fear and expectations of others was crucial; not owning the issues of others, whether it be their fear of particular situations or objects, or merely them being in a bad mood at the time. Regardless of the reasons, they are theirs not yours, and recognising and dismissing other people's concerns or judgments is an essential part of annihilating your stress and anxiety.

Feeling caught up in the expectations of others is something that we are all likely to encounter, whether it is in the workplace or socially. It is natural for everyone to have their mood swings, and we need to work out what is ours to own and what is somebody else's that we do not and should not own.

(*PEARLS* #13, 16)

Another realisation for Lauren regarding her thoughts about blood tests was that she needed to know exactly what was happening. Humans are curious by nature, and information is both powerful and important. If she broke the blood test scenario down into the small steps that happen throughout the procedure, she believed that she could manage quite well. From here she worked out a strategy for managing the entire routine, from arriving at the pathology center, to going into the pathology room, sitting in the chair, the procedure of the vials being prepared for the blood sample, the strap being placed on her arm, cleaning the skin, the needle being inserted and withdrawn. Lauren decided that if she knew when they were inserting the needle and they could use a countdown for her, she would manage it fine.

Having worked out her detailed strategy from leaving home, to arriving at the clinic, to the procedure and afterwards, Lauren then made an appointment for a blood test. She used *breathing* to assist her in remaining calm, even whilst making the appointment. She also focused on her rational and positive thinking. Most people who suffer severe stress and/or anxiety know that they are capable of rational thought and become frustrated with themselves when their emotional thinking takes over. So for Lauren, it was about staying calm enough to stay in control of her thinking. Putting her strategy in place, she arranged a blood test and spoke about her needs and proposed strategy to the nurse who was very cooperative and helpful. She managed the blood test procedure and was pleased with her efforts. She even celebrated afterwards by buying herself a bunch of flowers. This celebration was a sensible and positive step on Lauren's part. Congratulating oneself on all achievements, big or small, throughout the personal change process is an extremely important element in reinforcing the newly emerging positive mindset. Whilst recognising that there was still room for improvement regarding her stress and anxiety, Lauren felt she had made a breakthrough. Whilst it was unfortunate that she had previously experienced an unpleasant and distressing time with a blood test, it proved extremely useful for her to gain these insights into her needle phobia, which highlighted the role her thinking played in her fear responses. It has also highlighted the importance of sorting out which fears and behaviours are hers to own and deal with, and which belong to others.

(*PEARLS* #2, 13)

Lauren feels that she now has her needle phobia/stress management system in place, spearheaded by remembering her *breathing* and using that to check on her thinking. She uses *stop and breathe* when she needs to get her thinking back on track, and she has her routine that she outlines to the nurses when she has a blood test, which is working well for her.

She now needs to increase her comfort level (or lower her discomfort level) over time, by accepting the fact that having blood tests or needles might not be her favourite thing, but she will be okay. Her self-talk about the fact that you can sit with discomfort and still be okay is an important element in the ongoing management of stress. Lauren has done a great job of annihilating her stress and anxiety and now knows how to regain control of her emotions.

(*PEARLS* #1, 2, 13, 16)

These stories are examples of how different people have adapted various strategies to enhance their ability to manage their stress and anxiety, and by understanding how their issues escalated together with making changes to their thought processes and behaviours, they have re-established balance in their world.

Inner calm and focus
will strengthen the core
of your being.

Merryn Snare

“The greatest discovery of my generation is that a human being can alter his life by altering his attitudes of mind.”

William James

CHAPTER 10

Additional Treatment Methodologies

Whilst my primary focus for this book has been to create a handbook of techniques that you can implement yourself, there are a number of therapies in the healing and wellbeing field (as opposed to the strictly psychological field) that you may have heard of, wondered about, or were curious for some insight into their efficacy in dealing with stress and anxiety. The methodologies I have included in this chapter are all techniques for which I have trained, and I have used to some degree in my clinical work and whilst some of these techniques might seem fairly simple, I would suggest that initially, individuals should seek professional direction before adopting any of these strategies.

Hypnosis

What is it?

Austrian physician Franz Mesmer believed hypnosis was a magical flow of energy between the hypnotist and subject, and whilst this theory was quickly discounted, hypnosis was originally known as mesmerism[37]. We have probably all had experiences of being mesmerised by something; the feeling of total involvement in a thriller movie or drama series, being ensconced in a book, or transporting our mind to another place by staring at the flames of an open fire. It is as if we are there in our normal being or surroundings but also 'not there' at the same time. We can pull out of this space if we need or choose to but we can also enjoy the peace and serenity of being there. It is like we are giving ourselves the time, luxury and comfort of allowing our mind some down time.

Hypnosis is a process by which a clinician or therapist induces an altered state of attention or degree of awareness in the client[38]. There are many techniques that may induce this altered state or 'trance', including levitation, eye-roll, or relaxation, however, when I use hypnosis with clients I prefer a relaxation induction, as I believe learning a relaxation technique is an extremely useful strategy for everyone to learn and practice regularly.

For some, this altered state of consciousness occurs spontaneously, such as daydreaming or being mesmerised – taking the mind to a 'different place or plane' – whilst for others, this occurs as a result of the induction process. This difference in the ease with which one reaches the altered state may reflect an individual's belief about their 'hypnotisability', which in many cases reflects their ability to let go and relax. Some clients have reported that they have been told they are unable to be hypnotised, and there is indeed an assessment that some practitioners use to determine the likelihood of hypnotisabilty, and presumably the likely efficacy of using hypnosis as a tool in their treatment plan. A common concern for people who have observed or heard about hypnosis being used in the entertainment arena, is that they will behave in a manner that embarrasses them (such as squawking like a chicken), and together with the fear of losing control, they deem hypnosis too challenging to contemplate.

In a workshop for arachnophobia that I was involved with, a participant told the group that when he was at medical school they had undergone the hypnotisability test, and he was deemed to be 'unhypnotisable'. He went on to say that he found the hypnosis session that we had just completed had really surprised him, as he found himself relaxing and going to a place he had never thought possible.

Some people readily acknowledge their difficulty in relaxing, therefore believing hypnosis won't work for them and this alone is worth investigating. Is there something they fear letting go of, or are they are holding onto a belief that leads to their perception that they cannot be hypnotised? In such cases this may be a mindset issue. These factors have all contributed to my personal approach of using relaxation techniques as an induction for hypnosis, and since I work largely with people dealing with stress and anxiety issues, relaxation seems to be the best fit for my clients.

This does not mean that all people need to work through the modality of hypnosis, as there are numerous approaches for meeting people's needs. Furthermore, I would *never* consider using hypnosis with anyone who

was uncomfortable with the idea of it. For those who are interested however, it can be a powerful way of accessing thoughts and beliefs that have been locked in the subconscious or unconscious mind.

What happens?

Generally we think through our problems with our conscious mind; we consider every possible angle and go over and over things, eventually feeling like we are going around in circles. The subconscious mind holds accessible information that we are not necessarily focused on, but that can easily be brought to our immediate attention, such as if we are focused on listening to music as we travel home from work; our attention or conscious awareness might be on the music but we still have no trouble finding our way home. The unconscious mind is the automatic part of our thinking structure and is responsible for automatic parts of our functioning, such as breathing. The unconscious mind also holds beliefs and experiences that have accumulated since early childhood and which contribute to the development of 'who we are'. In essence, there are forces within the unconscious mind that drive our behaviours, and these forces may at times prove destructive[16]. By accessing our unconscious mind, we can usually find the answers to our recurring questions or ruminations and hypnosis is a strategy by which we can often achieve this more quickly.

Someone who has entered this altered state of consciousness is likely to experience a number of different phenomena, which may include alterations in consciousness or memory, increased susceptibility to suggestion, access to ideas unfamiliar in their normal state of mind, or changes in behaviour, perceptions and psychological processes. The state they reach is not sleep, nor is it like being under an anesthetic – it is more like the space between sleep and wakefulness. What is important to understand is that one is not unconscious when they are hypnotised. It is common however to feel relaxed and peaceful, with a sensation of lightness or floating. Contrary to some hearsay, one does *not* lose control

over their mind or feelings. In fact, the way psychologists describe it is that you always have a 'hidden observer' with you. Your hidden observer is there to monitor how the suggestions offered in the hypnosis fit with you personal ethos, and if you are asked to do anything that pushes your boundaries too far, your hidden observer will step in and ensure you are not breaching your personal ethics or compromising yourself in any way. Hence, hypnosis is natural, safe and is suitable for people of all ages when used by trained professionals.

How does it work?

Given that hypnosis transports the individual to a calm and relaxed space, it takes one beyond the conscious mind to a deeper level of cognition, and by working with the subconscious and unconscious mind, where all the underlying *belief structures* are stored, leaves the conscious mind out of the loop. Thus, the filtering or conscious control mechanism is bypassed. This provides scope for the creative and imaginative side of the individual to activate, perhaps in a way it has not done for a very long time. Not only does this enhance the individual's openness to new ideas and solutions, under the guidance of their hidden observer they may also be happy to participate in the child's play that we often see in the entertainment applications of hypnosis.

Thus, the individual is more open to following a stream of consciousness as suggested by the therapist, and is able to focus more on their inner-self than the external world. Reductions in hyper-vigilant monitoring of the outside world can lead to time distortions whilst engaged in hypnosis – people frequently think a 40 minute experience has only been five or ten minutes. They are also able to accept a greater level of incongruity in their logical thought process in hypnosis, whilst a heightened ability for selective inattention to irrelevant stimuli such as extraneous noises is common. There is a tendency to be less self-critical, with the conscious mind almost completely ignoring attempts at understanding or resolving

unhelpful thought processes. The state of 'letting go' in hypnosis is what paves the way for the individual to experience more vivid sensory imagery, as well as enhanced creativity and imagination, which together with a blurring of body and ego boundaries, enables the partial lifting of repressive barriers that may be dominating the conscious mind.

I should emphasise that in clinical hypnosis we *never* use this technique for entertainment. The clear distinction is in the word; hypnotists can lead one into trance and hypnotherapists use the technique for therapeutic benefit.

Once again, I reiterate the importance of seeking treatment from a professionally qualified practitioner.

What issues is hypnosis useful for?

It is possible to access hidden memories through hypnosis or in some cases, accessing more accurate details of those memories. However, hypnosis does not automatically improve memory. There can also be a distortion of memory, and in many situations what occurred for the client during hypnosis may fill in some gaps from the individual's conscious memory.

However, a key point here is that *recovered memories* via hypnosis are not admissible evidence in a court of law in Australia, and should there be a court case pending or likely at some time in the future, engaging in hypnosis may be detrimental to one's case. For this reason I do not use hypnosis if there is any hint of pending legal action.

Occasionally people might experience an abreaction in hypnosis. This might occur if a client accesses a deeply sensitive issue that has been completely blocked to their conscious awareness, and they may experience a physical reaction such as vomiting and nausea. This highlights the importance of seeking a qualified practitioner who can deal with such responses and restore the client's sense of safety.

There is a clear association between hypnosis and relaxation, and relaxation has a profound impact on stress and anxiety. Hence hypnosis, particularly with a relaxation induction, is beneficial for treating stress and anxiety, depression, motivational training and attitude change, sleep disorders, eating disorders, fears and phobias.

Pranic Healing

Pranic healing evolved from the work of Grand Master Choa Kok Sui, who, as a scientist and spiritual master, researched his theory over a period of 20 years[39]. Working in India and the Philippines, Grand Master Choa Kok Sui replicated his results sufficiently to warrant the formation of his healing technique known as Pranic healing. Prana is the Sanskrit word meaning 'life energy', and this approach to healing and wellbeing does not have a religious or sect connection, but rather is about energy or Prana, which in other cultures may be known as Qi (Chinese), Ki (Japanese), Mana (Polynesian), or Miwi (Aboriginal).

Dr Hazel Wardha, a homeopath from Melbourne who had a chance meeting with Grand Master Choa Kok Sui when visiting relatives in India, introduced Pranic healing to Australia. Dr Hazel had been unable to recover from the devastating and tragic loss of her son, and just before leaving India to return to Melbourne she heard about a lecture to be given by the Grand Master. Dr Hazel found that Pranic healing was the only therapy that assisted her in dealing with the enormity of her grief, and from there she went on to share the wonders that she had found with the rest of Australia and the South Pacific.

The premise of Pranic healing relates to how living things and beings transmit and receive energy, which is essential in maintaining balance of the mind, body and soul, and is helpful in enhancing general health across the physical, psychological, emotional and spiritual domains of the individual being. In essence, Pranic healing focuses on re-establishing balance of the mind, body and soul by cleansing, strengthening and

rebalancing the body and thus rectifying dis-ease within the body. The process can also be used to assist the health of animals and plants, and has also been applied to the balancing of relationships, finances, and general functioning within the workplace or home.

In 2003 Dr Hazel commissioned a study in conjunction with Japanese scientist and water specialist, Dr Masaru Emoto, where tap water was treated with Pranic healing[40]. By freezing the water and examining the crystals formed both before and after Pranic healing, photographs show amazing transformations of the crystals. Studies of water in bottles with different labels have also been conducted, and showed that negative words created the impact of murky water, whereas tranquil and heavenly words, such as the name of a goddess, created magnificent, clear crystals. Similarly, water exposed to heavy metal music developed a messy crystal structure, whilst water exposed to classical music showed beautifully intricate crystal structures. The purpose of this research was to see how and if Pranic healing could alter the state of organic matter, and, given their remarkable results, the contention was that since the energy mass that is our body is composed of 70% water, such influences must also impact the wellbeing of us as humans.

Dr Hazel has gone on to direct her energy into cellular regeneration as a result of these studies, and you can see further details of all of her research and find out more about Dr Hazel Wardha at the Ashish Institute for Inner Studies[40].

Emotional Freedom Technique (EFT)

EFT is an emotional healing technique that combines eastern and western medicine. It is based on the belief that negative emotions can be attributed to a disruption in the body's energy system[41,42]. EFT has been described as a treatment that lies somewhere between hypnosis, meditation and acupressure, and is often referred to as the psychological use

of the acupuncture meridians or *psychological acupressure*, i.e. the use of pressure points without needles. EFT is a useful technique to reduce the intensity of a negative feeling or the emotional response you experience in relation to a specific situation, and once the technique has been mastered, it is simple to implement.

Instead of using needles, one taps on energy points (largely around the face) to unblock and balance energy meridians that have become disrupted through thinking about an emotionally disturbing situation. Although the memory of the event remains, the balancing of the energy removes the emotionally charged response to the situation. Hence, EFT assists in restoring emotional balance by disconnecting the damaging negative thought, which might be likened to a different way of cutting the negative thought spiral. EFT is often referred to as 'tapping' because the technique is largely about tapping on the meridian points that activate the energy.

A relatively recent innovation, the discovery and resulting technique of EFT was developed by American psychologist, Roger Callahan, in the early 1980s[43]. Callahan was treating a client for water phobia when he made the link between meridians and the parts of the body that held the phobic response, in this case the stomach. Callahan realised that the pressure point associated with the stomach was under the eye, asked his client to tap that area, and before long she no longer experienced the dis-ease.

Gary Craig, who published his handbook on EFT in the late 1990s after working with numerous energy points that he found assisted with emotional issues, is also credited as being a founder of EFT[44,45]. He went on to develop a sequence of points that cover all meridians, finding positive results with a wide array of symptoms and diseases. Craig highlights that differing conditions require different timeframes for results, but his premise is that emotional distress can cause energy blockages, which is a significant factor in the cause of many physical diseases.

Relating this work to healing techniques from the east, we are largely aware that ancient healings of the Chinese and Indian cultures are focused on energy flow – the Qi or the Prana as mentioned previously. The techniques adopted in ancient healing address the clearing of blockages in the flow of such energy by working with the Qi and 12 meridians in the Chinese tradition, or using Prana to cleanse and heal the seven chakras in the Indian tradition. Hence, the notion that the stress symptoms we experience results in our bodies ending up in a state of imbalance or dis-ease, was formulated. Callahan's work also linked closely with the emerging popularity of applied kinesiology, which assesses muscle function via meridian points and sets out to unblock the meridians or nerve channels by tapping the points at their nerve endings, sending a pulse through the nerve to unblock the channel[45].

EFT is a safe, natural and gentle means of using one's own energy system to assist in healing emotional distress. It can be used for any difficult life situation including fear and phobia, post-traumatic stress, anger, sadness, stress or anxiety.

There are four main benefits of EFT:

1. *Relaxation* – this process, by virtue of the stress reduction, tends to leave participants feeling considerably more relaxed, as the damaging emotional response to the situation is disconnected.
2. Desensitises negative emotions and releases 'stuck' emotions.
3. Weakens the associated negative beliefs that underpin the problems.
4. With continued practice, the effect permeates to one's entire body and energy system, improving one's general outlook on life.

Scientific results of these 'alternative' therapies are less prevalent than studies within the medical, pure psychological (e.g. Cognitive Behavioural Therapy) or Chinese medicine domains. However they show some promising results[3].Just as the water crystal experiment conducted by Dr Hazel Wardha and Dr Masaru Emoto suggested an

amazing impact of Pranic healing on water, studies on samples of blood cells were found to be positively affected when EFT was used to clear negative emotions. Dr Patricia Felici, a doctor of clinical nutrition had noticed a patient's blood samples were clumped (not ideal for optimal health), but she found that after treating the patient with EFT the blood samples had improved in structure from the previous sample. In a bid to test this chance finding, Dr Felici and Gary Craig conducted both pre- and post-EFT trials on blood samples to determine whether emotions can affect the behaviour of blood cells. Their findings suggested astounding and positive improvements on the structure of blood cells[46,47]. Proponents of EFT believe it has benefits for the physical body as well as the emotional and psychological domains, given that it is the blocked energy flow that is the underlying cause of the emotional and psychological problems, which often leads to physical disease.

The EFT Process – Before You Start:

Determine what you are seeking to resolve. What is the negative feeling or emotional response that is causing discomfort and how is that making you feel? Observe the feeling and rate it on a scale of one to ten, where ten is very high or extreme, and one is very low or almost non-existent.

The Tapping Technique

Tapping Points

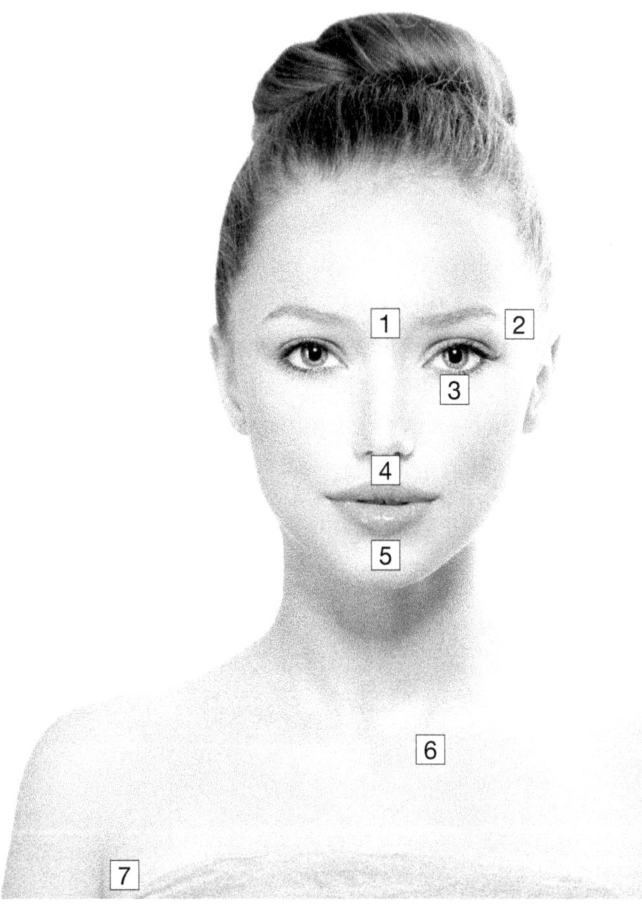

Tapping Points:

The diagram above illustrates where the tapping points are located. The *sore spot* is located between the shoulder and the collarbone, approximately in line with the boney V in the neck. When you gently rub the flat of your fingers over this area, you will notice a slightly raised part. It is also slightly tender when you use the circular motion.

1. Between the eyebrows
2. End of eyebrow
3. Under (the pupil of) the eye
4. Hollow under the nose
5. Hollow under the lip
6. Under one of the collarbone heads
7. Underneath armpit (3 centimetres down)

There is some variation in the meridians that different therapists use. All of the tapping points are useful but I am going to outline the sequence I have been taught and that I use in my clinical work.

It is important to find the correct point to tap – this is where it is a good idea to learn from a therapist initially. Alternatively, given that this technique is simple to use you can try it for yourself and if you are not noticing an improvement in the intensity of the feeling you are seeking to disengage, you can check out your technique with a professional who has undertaken EFT training.

- Tap gently as close to the meridian points as possible. Whilst you will succeed even if you are not exactly on the meridian, accuracy clearly leads to the best results.
- Tap the points with two fingers (the index and middle fingers – most people use their dominant hand, but either hand is fine) rather than one finger as it gives you more chance of hitting the right spot. Focus your thoughts on the problem as you tap and repeat your mantra.
- Tap seven to ten times on each point, but focus more on your thoughts than the number of taps. Ensure the tapping is hard enough to feel, but not so hard that it hurts.
- You can tap with either hand or on either side of your body or face.

Set-up statement:

Once you have decided what the feeling is that you are trying to disconnect from and how that emotion makes you feel, you need to have a statement or mantra to say to reinforce the energy release. This mantra should be focused on the essence of the emotional state you want to alter, and is always a variation on a basic theme:

"Even although I have this problem (e.g. I am scared of spiders) I am a good person"

OR

"I accept myself deeply and completely, even if I have this problem/feeling/difficulty/worry" (e.g. freak out at the thought of seeing a spider).

This mantra is said at the beginning of the tapping sequence whilst you gently rub the *sore spot* in a circular motion with your fingertips, with your fingers in an elongated, flat extension. Saying the statement aloud helps to reinforce the self-acceptance, so you might want to practice this technique in private!

Reminder phrase:

This is an abbreviated version of the set-up statement, repeated once at each of the seven tapping points e.g. *"this spider feeling"*.

Tapping sequence:

1. *Sore spot* – gentle circular motions and set-up statement, repeated three times.
2. Approximately seven taps on each meridian point, whilst saying the reminder phrase.
3. Repeat the entire sequence twice.

Regular practice is naturally going to enhance the long-term benefits gained from this technique, which is safe, natural and applicable to all age groups. This is another effective method of annihilating stress and anxiety.

> Our feelings reflect our thinking. Feelings are our first clue that our thoughts need checking.
>
> **Merryn Snare**

The Final Word

Now that we have discussed the significant elements that lead to the suffering caused by stress and anxiety, it is abundantly clear that mental health is the cornerstone of our general health and wellbeing. It is crucial that we look after it and take ownership and responsibility for it, which, on occasion, may require that we say no to requests from our family or loved ones when we know our personal resources are close to their limit.

I believe that there are two significant messages to take from this book. The first is about our thinking; the impact it has on our reactions to situations and how we experience the negative emotions relating to stress and anxiety. It is an awareness of where we are currently placed together with a direction for where we want to be, removing the thought patterns that currently fail us and establishing thoughts and beliefs that fit our enlightened being.

The second message is about the *PEARLS*; the 21 strategies that have been tried and tested by my clients. This is an array of strategies that cover different aspects of change and relate to different parts of one's daily routine. Try them out and see which *PEARLS* work for you, but most importantly, create your own resilience routine. Be diligent in practicing these strategies to ensure they become second nature in your response mechanism.

To review these strategies, I have listed my *PEARLS* below:

PEARLS for Immediate Relief:

1. Stop
2. Breathe
3. Visualise
4. Smile and laugh
5. Water – hydrate
6. Remove self – walk
7. Stretch

The Lifestyle PEARLS

8. Exercise regularly
9. Relaxation
10. Meditation
11. Sleep
12. Diet

PEARLS for Thinking About It

13. Talk/share – professionals
14. Self-talk/thoughts – reframe
15. Positive psychology
16. Acceptance

PEARLS of Personal Preference

17. Friends – social
18. Music
19. TV

The Essential PEARLS

20. Feed your energy
21. *The PEARLS of Resilience* – the formula to prevent *over-the-shoulder stress*

Whilst I encourage you to seek professional guidance if you are unable to sort out your mind matters or concerns, I also encourage you to develop your own toolkit of strategies. Choose the *PEARLS* that work for you and use them regularly to annihilate your stress and anxiety. Here's to a balanced life.

ABOUT THE AUTHOR

Psychologist, Teacher, Hypnotherapist, Speaker, and International Author

Merryn Snare has enjoyed a rewarding career as a registered psychologist, registered primary and special education teacher, dance therapist, bereavement and trauma counsellor, executive coach, author, world traveller, and mother.

At her core, Merryn believes in the power of deep relaxation to assist individuals with maintaining a sense of calmness, peace, and wellbeing. This belief is the common thread that ties together all of her professional pursuits.

Merryn combines her vast psychological and educational experience to help others achieve balance in their personal and professional lives. To her, the ultimate goal is a whole-life balance.

She has earned a Bachelor of Special Education, a Master of Psychology, a Graduate Diploma of Movement and Dance Therapy, and a Graduate Certificate of Dance Therapy. She is also trained in clinical hypnosis, eye movement desensitization and reprocessing, emotional freedom technique, mediation, and bereavement counselling.

Using her expertise, Merryn has worked with both intellectually disabled and autistic children as a classroom teacher, movement and dance teacher, and special language teacher. In this capacity, she introduced

the Makaton vocabulary and Auslan signing into special schools in Victoria. She has also served as a special education consultant in primary schools and as a Victorian Education Department representative on the Makaton Vocabulary Development Program Committee.

Much of Merryn's work centers on deep relaxation to help manage anxiety, phobias, and trauma. In addition to being interviewed on ABC radio about anxiety and arachnophobia, she has been a presenter in arachnophobia workshops held at the Melbourne Zoo, and a presenter at Anxiety Disorders Association Victoria workshops. She has also recorded four hypnosis CDs that help listeners sleep better without drugs, manage panic attacks, resolve their fear of flying, and stop smoking.

Always compassionate, Merryn counselled Bali bombing survivors in 2002, traffic monitoring staff and bridge workers after the Westgate Bridge tragedy in 2007, and those working to re-open roads after the 2007 Victorian bushfires – many of whom lost friends, family, and property in the fires.

As a part of her workplace assistance consulting that focuses on developing emotional intelligence and psychological awareness, Merryn has worked and consulted with leading brands such as RACV, VicRoads, the Australian Federal Police, the National Transport Commission, the Australian Dental Association, Royal Children's Hospital, the Country Fire Authority, the Transport Accident Commission, Victorian Workcover Authority, and the Education Department of Victoria, to name a few.

Merryn is the international Author of **"Annihilate Stress and Anxiety** *– 21 Proven Strategies for a Balanced Life"*

Merryn's professional affiliations include the Australian Psychological Society, the Anxiety Disorders Association of Victoria, the Mastering Business Acceleration Group, and the Institute of Teaching. This

collection of organizations gives Merryn continuing opportunities to share her experience and talents with the psychology and business community.

Embracing the richness of life and business, Merryn's travels have taken her to more than 25 countries, including Singapore, Malaysia, Thailand, Egypt, Ethiopia, Kenya, England, Scotland, France, Italy, Belgium, Spain, Cambodia, Vietnam, Indonesia, and Fiji. She has also travelled extensively throughout Australia.

Merryn lives in Melbourne Victoria Australia.

REFERENCES

1. Australian Psychological Society, Stress and wellbeing in Australia Survey, http://www.psychology.org.au/npw/survey/ (2013).
2. The Emily Post Institute, Stress, Rudeness and The American Workplace, http://www.boston.com/jobs/news/jobdoc/2013/11/stress_rudeness_and_the_americ.html (2013)
3. Costa, P.T. Jr. & McCrae, R.R. "Revised NEO Personality Inventory (NEO-PI-R) and NEO Five-Factor Inventory (NEO-FFI) manual." Psychological Assessment Resources, (1992).
4. Kerry L. Jang, W. John Livesley and Philip A. Vemon, "Heritability of the Big Five Personality Dimensions and Their Facets: A Twin Study." Journal of Personality, 64(3) (1996): 577-592.
5. Beck, A. T., http://www.beckinstitute.org/history-of-cbt/
6. Doige, N., The Brain that Changes Itself: Stories of Personal Triumph from the Frontiers of Brain Science (James H. Silberman Books, 2007).
7. Grant, M., Change Your Brain, Change Your Pain.(Mark Grant, 2009).
8. Skorucak, A., The Science of Tears , http://www.scienceiq.com/facts/scienceoftears.cfm
9. http://www.beyondblue.org.au/the-facts/anxiety/what-causes-anxiety
10. http://www.abc.net.au/health/library/stories/2005/06/07/1828950.htm, (2013)
11. DiTomasso, R.A. & Gosch, E.A. (Ed), Anxiety Disorders: A Practitioners Guide to Comparative Treatments, (Springer, New York, 2002).

12. http://www.hypoglycemia.asn.au/2011/anxiety-and-the-autonomic-nervous-system/ (2011)
13. Davis, B., "Healthy Relationships", http://www.huffingtonpost.com/bruce-davis-phd/healthy-relationships_b_3307916.html
14. McKay, M., Rogers, P. D. & McKay, J., When Anger Hurts, 2nd Ed., (New Harbinger, 2003).
15. Liebert, R. M. & Spiegler, M. D., Personality. Strategies and Issues. (Brooks/Cole, 1994).
16. Corsini, R. J. & Wedding, D. (Ed), Current Psychotherapies, (F.E. Peacock, Illinois, 1995).
17. James Harkness, "No lunch breaks or taking leave: health risks." Posted 26 Nov , 2013,http://www.workplaceinfo.com.au/
18. Smith, M. & Segal, J., "Laughter Is the Best Medicine," Posted February, 2014, http://www.helpguide.org/life/humor_laughter_health.htm
19. Otto, M. W. and Smits, Jasper, A. J., Exercise for Mood and Anxiety: Proven Strategies for Overcoming Depression and Enhancing Well-Being, Oxford University Press, 2011.
20. http://www.scientificamerican.com/article/why-do-you-think-better-after-walk-exercise/ (2013)
21. Mayo Clinic Staff, "Depression and Anxiety: Exercise eases symptoms," Posted 01 October, 2011, http://www.mayoclinic.org/diseases-conditions/depression/in-depth/depression-and-exercise/art-20046495
22. http://www.adaa.org/living-with-anxiety/managing-anxiety/exercise-stress-and-anxiety
23. Boone, T., "Benefits of Walking," Posted 18 April, 2014, http://health.howstuffworks.com/wellness/diet-fitness/exercise/benefits-of-walking5.htm

24. Sparacino, Alyssa "Eleven Surprising Health Benefits of Sleep," http://www.health.com/health/gallery/0,,20459221,00.html
25. "Good Nutrition for Mental Health – tips for individuals," http://www.workingcarers.org.au/index.php/work-n-care/health/1488-good-nutrition-for-mental-health--tips-for-individuals
26. Lakhan, S. E. & Vieir, K. F., "Nutritional therapies for mental disorders," Nutrition Journal, 7(2), (2008).
27. Royal College of Psychiatrists, "Eating well and mental health," Posted January, 2014, http://www.rcpsych.ac.uk/healthadvice/problemsdisorders/eatingwellandmentalhealth.aspx
28. Seligman, M. Learned Optimism: How to change your mind and your life, Simon and Schuster Audio, 1991, CD.
29. Hicks, E. & Hicks, J., The Law of Attraction CD Collection, Hay Audio, 2007, CD.
30. Dooley, M., Infinite Possibilities, (Atria Paperback, 2009).
31. Dooley, M., Manifesting Change: It Couldn't be Easier, (Atria Paperback, 2010).
32. Dooley, M., Leveraging the Universe, (Atria Paperback, 2011).
33. Ben-Shahar, T, "Positive Psychology," Lecture at Monash University Caulfield Campus, Melbourne, 2008.
34. Ben-Shahar, T., Happier (McGraw Hill, 2007).
35. McKinney, C.H., Antoni, M.H., Kumar, M., Tims, F.C. & McCabe, P.M. "Effects of guided imagery and music (GIM) therapy on mood and cortisol in healthy adults." Health Psychology 16, no. 4 (1997): 390-400.
36. "The Power of Music to Reduce Stress," PsychCentral, Posted 30 January, 2013, http://psychcentral.com/lib/the-power-of-music-to-reduce-stress/000930.
37. "History of Hypnosis," http://www.historyofhypnosis.org/

38. Australian Society of Hypnosis, http://www.hypnosisaustralia.org.au/
39. Master Choa Kok Sui, Miracles Through Pranic Healing, (Philippines, 1998).
40. Wardha, H., Emoto M., Exciting research experiment with Pranic Distant Healing, Posted 2014, http://www.aiis.com.au/index.php/pranic-healing/research
41. Wells, S. & Lake, D. Pocket Guide to Emotional Freedom (Waterford, 2001).
42. Wells, S & Lake, D., New Energy Therapies: Rapid change Techniques for Emotional Healing, (Steve Wells and Associates, 1999).
43. Callahan, R., "Thought Field Therapy," www.rogercallahan.com
44. Craig, G., "The Gold Standard for EFT," Posted 21 July, 2013, www.emofree.com
45. EFT Research, www.eftuniverse.com
46. Carrington, P., "EFT and Live Blood Under the Microscope," http://masteringeft.com/masteringblog/eft-and-live-blood-under-the-microscope/
47. "Before and after photos of Rouleaux," World Centre for EFT, Posted 1 December, 2009, http://www.danachivers-eft.com/emofree/Research/Research-other/rouleaux.htm.

Recommended Resources

ARE YOU LOOKING FOR AN EXPERT SPEAKER AND TRAINER AT YOUR NEXT CONFERENCE, FUNCTION OR TEAM DEVELOPMENT PROGRAM?

Whether your organization needs to motivate teams, boost workplace productivity and improve the overall bottom line, understanding the needs of your *people*, an organizations most valuable resource, is the best place to start.

Equipping your staff to manage the impact of stress, be it in their personal lives or within the workplace is the ideal starting point. Having an engaged and resilient workforce is your key to a healthy bottom line. Without this, no amount of equipment, processes or skills development will enable your teams to deliver to their true potential – and if your people can't achieve *their* true potential, nor can *your* business.

PRESENTATION FORMATS

Keynote

This engaging presentation will leave your participants energized and excited about the information they have just learned.

Please allow 1–2 hours

Full Day or Half Day Workshops

These programs are tailored to suit the outcomes and objectives of your organization. Using exercises, activities and group experiences, these workshops enable insight and awareness of personal growth, and provide practical strategies to build resilience among participants. This not only develops personal wellbeing but enhances team effectiveness and workplace morale. Participant manuals are provided.

For further details visit our website
www.ResilienceBrilliance.com.au

StressFree Solutions

OFFERING A RANGE OF PRODUCTS TO ASSIST IN DE-STRESSING YOUR WORLD

Whether you need help with troublesome sleep patterns, mindset mastery, or support in managing your stress responses, the StressFree Solutions range can assist you in establishing balance in your life. These products have been developed by Merryn Snare and include self-study programs, audio CD's and books. They will enable you to tap into Merryn's wealth of knowledge and experience, and use the strategies that have assisted many people in overcoming their concerns in a practical and stress-free manner.

Visit the website to view the full range of products.
www.AnnihilateStressAndAnxiety.com.au

Leishman Financial Services is a second generation family business focussed on financial counselling to provide help peace of mind to clients. Simone & Chris Vanden-Driesen have been advising with Leishman Financial Services since 1993 and 1997 respectively. They work with clients to help build financial independence and security. Working with retirees and pre-retirees Simone and Chris can help you with budgeting, superannuation, life insurance, and retirement planning issues. Both have extensive experience assisting in Aged Care funding advice as well as Centrelink.

At Leishman Financial Services they say "Our family looking after your family" and that's exactly what happens. Advice on Aged Care will involve working with the elderly client's family members to achieve the most suitable solution for both care and financial constraints.

They work with young families to put in place life insurance, accident and income insurance policies in case one of life's traumatic events is thrown your way. Such policies can be the difference between your family being secure in the event of your death, or being forced out of their home.

Peace of mind cannot be bought, with but with sound financial advice, you can take the financial burden out of your life.

Highly qualified and experienced, the advisers at Leishman Financial Services will help you with all of your financial planning needs.

info@leishmans.com.au www.leishmans.com.au
Ph: +61 3 9561 9699
Level 4 / 295 Springvale Road Glen Waverley 3150

Cooper Newman
Real Estate
Reliable property advice

255 Burwood Highway
Burwood, Victoria 3125
03 9831 9831
cnre.com.au

Cooper Newman Real Estate is an agency built on the foundation of undertaking business within an ethical environment. Sometimes the easiest way to do business is to tell people what they want to hear. This frequently results in half truths, or even outright lies.

We believe if our staff are sufficiently skilled, the truth can be relayed *and* the best result for the client can be achieved with minimal stress.

As a result, we *guarantee* our work and operate on the basis that no money whatsoever is to be paid without a sale. This leaves the risk where it ought to be – with the agent who represents his or herself as a professional.

ADDITIONAL RESOURCES

Australian Psychological Society – http://www.psychology.org.au/

Anxiety Disorders Association of Victoria (ADAVIC) – www.adavic.org.au/

Beyond Blue – www.beyondblue.org.au/

Sane Australia – www.sane.org/

Lifeline – www.lifeline.org.au/ PH: 13 11 14

Mind Health Connect – http://www.mindhealthconnect.org.au Ph:1800 022 222

www.ingramcontent.com/pod-product-compliance
Ingram Content Group UK Ltd.
Pitfield, Milton Keynes, MK11 3LW, UK
UKHW020141250726
13967UKWH00002B/802